INVESTING
OFFSHORE

INVESTING OFFSHORE

Peter Sabourin
David Schincariol
Alec McLennan

Self-Counsel Press
(a division of)
International Self-Counsel Press Ltd.
U.S.A. Canada

Self-Counsel Press acknowledges the financial support of the
Government of Canada through the Book Publishing Industry
Development Program for our publishing activities.
Printed in Canada.

First edition: November 1998

Canadian Cataloguing in Publication Data

Sabourin, Peter.
Investing offshore

ISBN 1-55180-204-X

1. Investments, Foreign — Handbooks, manuals, etc.
I. Schincariol, David, 1972- II. McLennan, Alec. III. Title.
HG4538.S29 1998   332.2'73   C98-910621-7

Self-Counsel Press
(a division of)
International Self-Counsel Press Ltd.

1704 N. State Street	1481 Charlotte Road
Bellingham, WA 98225	North Vancouver, BC V7J 1H1
U.S.A.	Canada

CONTENTS

PART II — OFFSHORE LOCATIONS

TABLES

FIGURES

NOTICE TO READERS

This book provides an overview of offshore investment options and is not intended nor should it be considered to be a legal treatise. It furthermore does not offer an opinion as to the validity under the laws of any jurisdiction of any specific method which might be selected to implement a strategy. Rather, it is an attempt to highlight that the use of offshore centers is legitimate and that they can provide many opportunities to individuals and corporations in their international business, tax, asset protection, investment, and estate planning needs.

Laws are constantly changing. Every effort is made to keep this publication as current as possible. However, the author, the publisher, and the vendor of this book make no representation or warranties regarding the outcome or the use to which the information in this book is put and are not assuming any liability for any claims, losses, or damages arising out of the use of this book. The reader should not rely on the author or the publisher of this book for any professional advice.

ACKNOWLEDGMENTS

We would like to express our appreciation to the many international institutions, government agencies, accounting and legal firms, and Sabourin and Sun Inc.'s Toronto office and affiliates and staff who have contributed to making this book as thorough and complete as possible.

We would specifically like to express our appreciation to Kevin Fabian, Sabourin and Sun's research and compliance associate, and Greg Irwin, who have been integral to the compilation of this text.

Thank you also to Saverio Manzo of the Royal Bank Financial Group and to various members of the University of Toronto, London School of Economics, and Harvard Business School.

INTRODUCTION

Over the last few years, many individuals and corporations have asked us how they can legally use offshore vehicles to operate their businesses or manage their finances safely and profitably. This book has been created for the professional, business manager, business owner, private investor, and the average person, whatever his or her background or interest. It was inspired by the growing demand for information about how to improve investment returns, protect assets, develop profitable international business opportunities, plan personal estates, and reduce tax burdens.

Using offshore vehicles can offer all these advantages, allowing for improved investment and business growth. An offshore structure can be set up in a number of ways, and the type of structure you choose will depend on what business or financial needs you have. Some common components of an offshore structure include:

- **corporate** and **personal bank accounts,***
- offshore corporations (e.g., international business companies),
- trusts,

---

*Glossary terms are bold when they first appear in the text.

- foundations, and
- offshore banks.

All these elements are discussed in the chapters that follow.

Most individuals and corporations are not aware that there are perfectly legal ways to invest offshore. Many Canadian and U.S. companies legitimately use international tax treaties to reduce their tax payable from as high as 45% or 50% to as low as 2.5%. You can use offshore vehicles to reduce or even eliminate some of your taxes, which will give you significantly higher compounded rates of return. Increased investment options and the tax-free nature of many offshore investments mean that offshore portfolios can grow up to 2.3 times faster than onshore ones. For example, a conservative portfolio of $100,000 with no on-going investment, growing for ten years at 15% per year, could be worth $350,000 offshore versus just under $200,000 onshore. This is because of both increased investment choice and reduced tax rates. This makes a big difference if you are planning for your retirement.

As offshore service providers reduce the costs and complexities of accessing international financial centers, an increasing number of North Americans are restructuring the ownership of their personal and business assets to plan their estates and take advantage of superior investments, asset protection, and legal tax reduction. At the same time, trade and business continue to grow globally. Many business owners and senior managers are turning to offshore for tax advantages and business and investment opportunities. Whether you are an individual or a corporation, offshore centers offer a wide variety of advantages. This book can help you design an effective and legal plan to benefit from them.

Part I of this book outlines and explains the options and advantages of using offshore financial centers for both individuals and corporations. Part II provides detailed descriptions of several of the best offshore jurisdictions: each jurisdiction's advantages, areas of specialty, and the laws that affect individuals and corporations. All dollar amounts are in U.S. dollars unless otherwise stated. There is also a chapter of frequently asked questions and a detailed glossary. Glossary terms are in bold when they first appear in the text.

This book explains the process of doing business and investing offshore. It will help individuals and businesses structure offshore investments, but it's best to also get professional assistance for your particular case. Planning your offshore investment strategy requires the use of competent, experienced professionals who are knowledgeable in both domestic and international laws and who also will consider your personal or business financial objectives when advising you. Readers should consult their accountant or lawyer or, preferably, a specialized offshore service provider.

PART I

INVESTING
OFFSHORE

1
WHAT IS OFFSHORE?

a. WHY GO OFFSHORE?

With the rapid growth in the number of offshore centers, why aren't more U.S. and Canadian individuals and corporations investing offshore? One reason is that using offshore jurisdictions is a relatively complicated process that is best done with the guidance of a reputable, experienced offshore advisor.

Another reason offshore centers are not used is that many people are simply not aware of the advantages of offshore investing. Some of the broad benefits of structuring your affairs offshore include:

- Tax planning
- Improved investment returns
- Access to global markets and investments
- Asset protection
- Diversification and risk management
- Economic and political security
- Estate planning
- Confidentiality and privacy
- Currency protection
- Pre-immigration planning

b. WHAT DOES OFFSHORE MEAN?

The term **offshore** refers to a practice in which some or all of an investor's financial activities are in a jurisdiction other than where the investor lives. These activities are not necessarily located on an island in the Caribbean Basin, though. For Canadian and U.S. residents, any financial services accessed outside Canada or the United States are considered offshore. For example, a Canadian or U.S. resident who opens a bank account in Austria has set up an offshore bank account.

Offshore includes a number of different types of activities. You might be familiar with it being used to describe banking or investing. In this book, the term is also used to encompass all the different activities to which the description "offshore" can apply.

c. THE ORIGINS OF OFFSHORE FINANCIAL CENTERS

The extensive and widespread use of offshore services by individuals and small **corporations** is relatively new. Fortune 1000 and globally oriented businesses have been accessing these services for decades, and getting enormous benefits and strategic advantages from them. However, offshore options were usually too expensive for most individuals and small businesses to use. Now, this is changing.

Forty years ago, there were only a handful of offshore centers, and few professionals specializing in offshore practice. The relatively low numbers of both offshore **jurisdictions** and professionals capable of providing access to them were compounded with technical limitations as well. As a result, the costs and complexities of offshore investing were considerable and often excessive. Offshore also suffered from a lack of public understanding. Sometimes offshore attracted people who were engaging in disreputable activities and who found it difficult to carry out such undertakings onshore. These people would choose offshore because its advantages included privacy, **asset protection**, and tax reduction. Their abuse of these advantages gave offshore a bad reputation.

Over the last 20 years, advances in technology and telecommunications have made offshore facilities more cost-effective and easier to use. A center in one location can now link up with other centers across great distances without large expenses. Many governments have recognized the opportunities available to offshore financial centers and have promoted their jurisdictions as conscientious offshore business centers. Changes in the legislation of these jurisdictions and improved controls for security and confidentiality have made offshore jurisdictions safe, secure, and accessible for legitimate businesses and investors.

Offshore centers have gradually become an acceptable component of normal business activity. They are used globally, 24 hours a day, seven days a week, by multinational corporations, domestic companies, professionals, and private investors. Offshore is now a clearly defined option individuals and businesses can use to legally reduce their tax burdens. Since offshore centers also offer high returns on investment, assured confidentiality, financial privacy, and increased business opportunities, there has been a dramatic growth in offshore financial market operations. Competitive and accessible offshore centers have developed into major global businesses. Offshore transactions currently account for approximately half of the world's financial transactions.

d. ADVANTAGES OF OFFSHORE

Offshore has many advantages and benefits that are not necessarily available through onshore financial centers. Some of these advantages are discussed below. However, this list is not exhaustive. Your financial advisor should be able to describe all the benefits available to you.

1. Tax minimization

Tax is the most significant cost of doing business and the largest factor determining a portfolio's compounded rate of return, so individuals and corporations have good reason to seek ways of legally minimizing their taxes. Table 1 shows approximate tax rates of some high-tax countries. These are potential tax rates payable for high net-worth individuals. Similarly high rates of tax may apply to corporations.

Many offshore centers have links with high-tax countries, providing tax savings not available in the high-tax countries. Such centers are effective, legitimate vehicles for minimizing taxes on investment income and capital appreciation. Through carefully structured international investment planning, investments can grow tax-free, uninterrupted by government taxes.

TABLE 1: TAX RATES FOR HIGH NET-WORTH INDIVIDUALS

HIGH-TAX COUNTRIES	CAPITAL GAINS TAX (%)	DIVIDEND TAX (%)	INCOME TAX (%)
Australia	35	35	42
Canada	53 (of 75%)	38	53
France	35	55	55
Germany	0	52	52
Italy	25	55	55
Japan	65	35	60
U.K.	40	0	40
U.S.	39	39	35

2. Expanded investment opportunities

Investment opportunities expand dramatically when you invest offshore. If you invest in several markets, low performance in one offshore market may be offset by high performance in other markets. Global diversification can also offer the potential for high returns and long-term stability. When you add global investments to your portfolio, you can both decrease risk and improve investment performance.

Onshore banks often have many regulations and structures that increase operating costs and reduce the rates of return they can offer investors. In contrast, offshore banks feature reasonable, self-imposed regulations and increased investment mobility. The results are superior opportunities for investment and diversification. Chapter 6 discusses global investing in more detail.

3. Asset protection

Offshore centers may protect your assets from the threat of lawsuits, bankruptcy, political instability, or future legislation that might adversely affect your family's or corporation's financial well-being. Such legislation may include a government's decision to change or impose currency **exchange controls** (controls to prevent or limit the fluctuation of a currency's value), death and inheritance taxes, gift taxes, or capital transfer taxes. See chapter 7 for more information on asset protection.

4. Estate planning

Offshore centers offer estate-planning advantages not found in high-tax countries such as the United States and Canada. These centers are excellent locations to hold investments, family assets, and estate property because they allow investment income to accumulate tax-free. This income can provide for, or eventually be passed on to, designated beneficiaries with minimal tax liability. Estate planning is discussed further in chapter 7.

5. Confidentiality

As global business and access to advanced technology have expanded, frivolous lawsuits and corporate espionage have also increased. There is a growing need for security and privacy within international business dealings. Offshore centers are an excellent way to ensure financial privacy and confidentiality because there is minimal government intrusion in your personal financial activities and bank-client interactions. Your home jurisdiction does not have records of these transactions. Anyone who tries to breach this confidentiality will have to go through a long, often arduous, process. Offshore centers want to preserve their reputation as confidential locations and therefore usually refuse demands for disclosure from other jurisdictions.

An offshore company incorporated in a jurisdiction such as the British Virgin Islands will enjoy a very high degree of protection because of the British Virgin Islands' policy of nondisclosure. The combination of an offshore corporation and an offshore **trust** will make it virtually impossible for anyone even to identify the ultimate owner of the company or the benefactor of the trust (the person who will one day be the beneficiary of the trust and all its assets). The beneficial owner's interests are secure and protected.

If you properly and legally set up your **offshore structure**, paper trails from legal business transactions are not a concern because your privacy and confidentiality are already assured and your offshore structure properly deals with onshore tax issues. Many times, offshore investors may seek to eliminate a paper trail to avoid frivolous lawsuits. However, it is possible to transfer assets without a paper trail to further protect privacy and confidentiality.

e. TYPES OF OFFSHORE JURISDICTIONS

Many jurisdictions outside Canada and the United States offer significant legal tax advantages as offshore centers. Some countries have no direct taxation, and others do not tax income from foreign sources or have relatively low tax levels. Some countries offer special tax privileges for particular activities, and some have signed tax treaties with high-tax jurisdictions such as Canada, the United States, or Britain which permit their use as tax havens.

1. No-tax jurisdictions

Some countries do not impose any personal or corporate income taxes, capital gains taxes, or wealth taxes. Individuals or corporations can incorporate a company or form a trust in these jurisdictions. The governments of these countries earn some revenue from the fees they charge for incorporation or trust formation, but what you as an individual or corporation would pay in fees is generally a fixed fee and is negligible when compared to what you would be paying in taxable jurisdictions. Government revenues include small fees on documents of incorporation, small charges on the value of corporate shares, and annual registration fees. Popular no-tax jurisdictions are the Bahamas, Bermuda, and the Cayman Islands.

Individuals or corporations looking for the highest possible level of privacy and confidentiality for their transactions prefer no-tax jurisdictions. Such jurisdictions are also attractive to investors with small- to mid-sized portfolios, for two main reasons. Setting up an offshore structure in a no-tax jurisdiction is relatively inexpensive. As well, no-tax jurisdictions generally have the lowest annual maintenance costs when compared with the other three types of jurisdictions. Investors with portfolios starting at $100,000 will find significant tax, asset protection, and **estate planning** advantages in no-tax jurisdictions.

2. No-tax-on-foreign-income jurisdictions

Jurisdictions such as Hong Kong, Austria, and the British Virgin Islands do not impose any form of income taxes on individuals or corporations if the income is obtained through foreign sources. This income cannot involve any local business activities apart from simple administration. If you obtain income from local sources, relevant income taxes apply.

Other no-tax-on-foreign-income jurisdictions include Gibraltar, Guernsey, the Isle of Man, Panama, and Jersey. No-tax-on-foreign-income jurisdictions fall into two classes. The first class allows a corporation or individual to conduct both foreign and domestic business but pay tax only on income obtained from domestic sources. The second class provides tax exemption to companies that engage exclusively in foreign business. No-tax-on-foreign-income jurisdictions require a company to decide at the time of its incorporation whether it will engage in local business, with the consequent tax liabilities, or whether it will engage in foreign business only, which would make it exempt from taxation.

While individual investors are still attracted to no-tax-on-foreign-income jurisdictions, many find that the annual operating costs in these jurisdictions are higher than in other types of jurisdictions.

3. Low-tax jurisdictions

Low-tax jurisdictions — Barbados, Switzerland, or Luxembourg, for example — impose *some* taxes on all income, wherever and however it is earned. Many of these jurisdictions have **double-taxation treaties**, as does Cyprus, with high-tax countries such as Canada and the United States. These treaties may reduce the **withholding tax** that high-tax countries impose on income an individual or corporation earns in the high-tax countries, or one country may give you credit for another's tax already paid.

Low-tax jurisdictions attract mainly corporate international business. Their setup and maintenance costs are higher than in no-tax and no-tax-on-foreign-income jurisdictions. However, their **treaty** networks and specific laws attract corporations with a specific agenda, such as leasing equipment, conducting international finance, or offering foreign market public listings.

4. Unique-tax jurisdictions

Unique-tax jurisdictions impose a regular range of taxes. However, they may provide special concessions. These might include total exemption from tax for shipping companies, movie-production operations, and financial companies. Concessions might also be available for specific forms of corporate organization, such as the uniquely flexible corporate arrangements offered in Liechtenstein. The Netherlands and Austria also offer similar kinds of specialized arrangements.

Unique-tax jurisdictions tend to attract high net-worth investors, individuals who have complicated asset protection or estate planning needs, as well as corporations.

f. COMMON OFFSHORE INVESTMENT STRUCTURES

An offshore corporation, such as an **international business company** (IBC), could have an offshore bank account anywhere in the world. If properly structured, with signing authority for the account clearly specified, funds can be utilized without incurring any tax or reporting requirements. Similarly, an offshore corporation could set up investment accounts anywhere in the world that, if you structure them properly, you could direct without incurring any tax. Corporate credit and debit cards allow access to offshore funds from anywhere in the world.

It is not unusual to use a combination of offshore structures to achieve your personal or business objectives.

Canadian and U.S. individuals or corporations commonly combine an offshore corporation and **trust** to protect their assets. Either personally or as part of a corporation, you may decide to set up an offshore trust that owns an offshore corporation with **bearer shares** (a type of share that allows ownership to transfer with relative anonymity). Instead of owning the assets or corporation yourself, the trust — an entity which is legally distinct from you — owns the assets or corporation. Although you or your heirs may become discretionary beneficiaries of the trust, you do not legally own the trust or assets at present.

Establishing separate legal ownership of assets is fundamental to offshore practices. Distinct legal ownership can reduce taxes and remove onshore or corporate legal liability. Figure 1 shows the relationships between an IBC and a trust. It is important to realize that the IBC and the trust create a legal liability loop. The trust assets are composed of the IBC's bearer shares, so the trust owns the IBC. In addition, the IBC established the trust so that you are not legally responsible for the trust.

FIGURE 1: COMMON OFFSHORE CORPORATE STRUCTURE

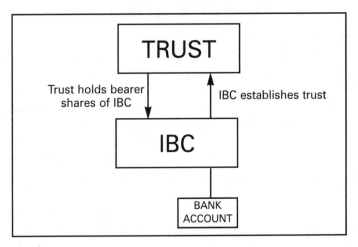

Because you are taxed on your worldwide personal income, the primary benefit for you in the combination of corporation and trust is that the trust is the sole owner of the company. Even though you or your heirs may be future beneficiaries of the trust (at the discretion of the trustee), profits are *not* going directly to you. Instead, they may accumulate tax-free in an offshore bank account. However, if you receive funds from either the company or the trust, and the funds are paid onshore as income, capital gains, or dividends, then tax becomes due generally, although depending on local laws, there may be some exemptions such as tax-free capital gains or dividend income from a qualified immigrant trust.

There are many legal ways of ensuring that you retain control over your corporate affairs, that your affairs remain confidential, and that onshore reporting is eliminated, while still saving tax. These ways are discussed in detail throughout this book. However, you should make your plans with the help of a reputable financial advisor.

g. MAKING THE MOVE OFFSHORE

Most people move offshore one step at a time. This way, they can build up their comfort level for new, unfamiliar business and investment strategies. The move offshore does not need to happen all at once, nor does it mean that onshore activities are no longer useful. You will maximize the advantages of offshore structures when you use offshore corporations, trusts, or bank accounts *with* onshore corporations or assets.

If you are looking to invest offshore, you might consider the following steps. To comply with the onshore tax and **reporting laws** of your resident country, you may want to structure an offshore international business company and trust through foreign **corporate bank accounts**. An IBC does not have the same reporting requirements as an onshore individual or corporation. Properly structured, the

IBC can invest offshore, tax free. However, you may find that there is a business onshore that is a good investment. The offshore IBC can now invest in this onshore business because to the IBC, your home country is a foreign jurisdiction. This is a common procedure among business owners who incorporate offshore to let their personal assets grow, and then decide to take their onshore company public.

If the IBC owns the shares of your onshore company, you can reduce tax. You can also use this arrangement for asset protection and estate planning.

As you become more comfortable with the advantages and uses of offshore, you will find that there are more and more opportunities for combining your offshore and onshore efforts.

h. THE LEGALITY OF INVESTING

Many individuals and corporations use offshore structures. When properly implemented and maintained, offshore centers and services are legitimate, flexible investment options. Tax authorities generally agree that you have the right to structure your business and personal activities so that you pay the minimum possible taxes under the law and have the right to invest your money anywhere in the world. They also respect the legal use of offshore financial centers to reduce taxes. If you use offshore to restructure your income, you can legally avoid certain taxes. **Tax evasion**, however, is an illegal means of reducing tax liability and is dealt with severely.

Tax rules attack only abusive tax schemes — schemes that obtain tax benefits contrary to the law or that circumvent its purpose. They do not prevent or interfere with legitimate commercial and personal transactions. Many governments will more willingly accept and recognize your offshore activities if you can demonstrate that your offshore agenda is motivated by factors other than tax reduction (e.g., asset protection, estate planning, or business purposes).

The United States Internal Revenue Service (IRS) and Revenue Canada each define over 30 locations around the world as offshore financial centers or tax havens, including Austria, the Cayman Islands, Hong Kong, Liechtenstein, Panama, Singapore, and Switzerland, as well as lesser-known places such as Bahrain, Grenada, Nauru, the Turks and Caicos Islands, and Vanuatu. Part II of this book provides a detailed description of several offshore financial centers.

The IRS and Revenue Canada do not target you unfairly if you operate within the parameters of the law and respect the reporting laws that affect you. Remember that it is *your* responsibility to report your offshore activities where legally required. Ignorance of the laws or failure to report the appropriate information could result in severe consequences. You should always be informed and aware of the laws and of their relevance to your specific situation. These laws include:

- Currency reporting rules
- Anti-avoidance rules
- Foreign property reporting rules
- Taxation of foreign income rules
- Attribution rules
- Accrual of property income laws

A qualified offshore service provider should be able to help you determine which laws apply to your specific business or situation.

Over the past 15 years, Canada has entered into many tax treaties with offshore centers, all aimed at curbing tax evasion. Recent changes to the tax rules for Canadian residents' investment income have also demonstrated a determined effort on the part of the federal government to tighten the tax net and collect more taxes from foreign sources of income. Because of this, you must properly set up your off-shore structures and comply with both the domestic and foreign corporate and tax laws.

Similar changes have occurred in the United States. These changes have had considerable publicity and some criticism, particularly from recent immigrants who are concerned about the intrusive nature of the revised reporting requirements. Canadian and U.S. resident individuals, corporations, or trusts are currently taxed on worldwide income from all sources, including employment income, business income, property gains, and capital gains.

Simply knowing what a government's general approach to offshore is, is not enough to ensure your offshore activities comply with the relevant laws. Laws change and individual situations vary and evolve. It is best to consult an offshore professional, lawyer, or accountant to ensure your plans are appropriate and legal. Individuals and corporations should find that they can accomplish their personal or business objectives without taking risks or hiding their legitimate activities from lawmakers.

i. WHAT DOES THE FUTURE HOLD FOR OFFSHORE?

Increasing demand for offshore facilities over the last 20 years has resulted in a growing number of offshore centers, all competing fiercely with one another for business. During 1997, more than 85,000 offshore companies were formed in the Caribbean. When European and Pacific offshore jurisdictions are included, the cumulative number of companies formed exceeded 160,000 for the year. Conservative estimates suggest that by the turn of the century, another 500,000 offshore companies will have been incorporated worldwide.

The offshore location of choice is currently the British Virgin Islands, where the registrar has incorporated approximately 320,000 IBCs in the last ten years. During 1997, roughly 62,000 IBCs were incorporated there.

Offshore investors demand high-quality service at a reasonable cost, access to sophisticated investment services, and confidentiality. Tomorrow's offshore users will continue to insist on these features, looking for financial centers that can compete in the following ways:

- Attractive and reliable regulatory environment
- Well-developed communications network
- Jurisdictional specialization
- Impeccable credibility
- Well-developed infrastructure
- Stable political and economic systems
- Expertise in international financial services
- Flexibility in design and use
- Easy accessibility

Competition and proliferation alone will not account for the growth of offshore centers. Political and economic catalysts will also influence the growth of the offshore industry in the next century. Some of these factors may be —

- Excessive taxation levels within the United States and Canada
- Political and economic instability within both offshore and onshore regions
- Continued market globalization and deregulation of trade
- Internationalization of business
- Lifting of trade barriers (e.g., EEC, NAFTA, APEC)
- Global lifting of exchange controls
- Creation of and effects of changes to double-taxation treaties and trade agreements

We predict the following trends will also influence the continued worldwide growth of offshore centers:

- Rapid economic change in the Asian-Pacific trading region

- Restructuring of former communist countries following the end of the Cold War
- Emergence of Brazil, India, and China as global economic powers
- Volatility in global currency markets as more countries move to free-trading currencies and the U.S. dollar becomes the global benchmark

While no one knows exactly how these factors will affect offshore activities, offshore will certainly continue to grow and develop as a viable and effective option for sound financial planning.

2
PRIVATE AND CORPORATE GLOBAL BANKING

The most common reason individuals and corporations access offshore centers is for commercial and private banking services. In the Bahamas, for example, banking employs over 3,000 people. The predominance of offshore banking in jurisdictions like the Bahamas is primarily because of advantageous banking laws that ensure good service, confidentiality, and asset and tax protection. These laws also provide freedom from certain banking regulations. Offshore banks often do not have reserve requirements or strict treasury laws. As a result, they can lend funds at lower interest rates and pay higher rates on deposits. They also have more freedom than onshore banks to invest depositors' funds, and can provide attractive investment returns on relatively low-risk bonds, term deposits, and other bank products.

a. BANKING SECRECY

Banking secrecy is the foundation of global private banking. A banker's obligation to maintain strict confidentiality is based on your rights to personal protection and privacy.

These basic rights are outlined in many countries and in the United Nations' human rights act. However, the introduction of intrusive fiscal laws, severe limitations to how capital can be transferred, and the existence of digital transactions has resulted in a significant loss of privacy for legitimate business and private financial matters. Many offshore jurisdictions have laws forbidding anyone to divulge a banking secret that he or she has been entrusted with. The punishment can be a fine — sometimes as much as millions of dollars — or imprisonment. Government authorities can spontaneously initiate proceedings against an offender, even if there has been no complaint or denunciation.

Banking secrecy is preserved in two ways: imposed secrecy or self-imposed secrecy. Imposed secrecy refers to bank secrecy legislation, often found in a jurisdiction's bank act and usually administered and policed by a central bank or minister of finance. Self-imposed bank secrecy involves an individual bank's adoption of additional secrecy requirements outside of a bank act.

An offshore bank's ability to provide secrecy and discretion is extremely important. The right to banking secrecy belongs exclusively to the client (personal or corporate), not to the bank. Banking secrecy can be lifted only if a client is first convicted of a criminal offense such as money laundering, insider trading, or drug trafficking. Most offshore jurisdictions do not consider tax-related infractions criminal offenses.

Secrecy extends far beyond keeping account content and ownership confidential. Ideally, it includes the ability to engage in discreet bank transactions and services. Secrecy has never amounted to blanket protection. By law, banking secrecy protects the public's interests and prevents any unjust interference in these interests.

b. SERVICES TO LOOK FOR IN AN OFFSHORE BANK

1. Banking laws

The offshore bank you choose should be in a jurisdiction whose banking laws suit your agenda. In the absence of rigid or well-defined bank laws, look for a bank that has taken the initiative to define its own set of regulatory practices.

2. Level of disclosure

Banks usually ask their clients to provide certain confidential details, such as jurisdictions of residence, bank references, and sources of funds. The level of disclosure that a bank requires may determine if you are prepared to work with that institution. Establish a sense of what information you are willing to disclose to your offshore bank and check to make sure that your boundaries will be respected both initially and throughout the duration of your interactions.

3. Deposit expectations

When you choose an offshore bank, consider its deposit expectations. Typically, banks that set high minimum deposits will provide superior service — but they require large deposits to maintain an account. If you choose a bank with low minimum-deposit requirements, make sure you will still receive optimum service.

4. Bank insurance

Depending on your agenda, you may need an insured bank, although there are a number of bank acts in place. For example, the United Kingdom Depositors' Act requires its banks to insure depositors' investments to varying amounts depending on the circumstances. If you intend to leave significant assets in a bank, it is recommended that you choose an insured bank.

c. ADVANTAGES OF OFFSHORE BANKS OVER LOCAL BANKS

Private offshore banks provide better service than onshore banks in most respects. But before you choose an offshore bank, do some research. Make sure the bank is reputable and willing to work with you as opposed to simply acting as a reservoir for your deposits. Choose your bank based on service, reputation, and its ability to communicate well with you. Table 2 is a general comparison of local and offshore banks, and suggests some factors you may want to consider when evaluating your potential offshore bank.

TABLE 2: COMPARISON OF LOCAL AND OFFSHORE BANKS

FEATURES	LOCAL BANK	OFFSHORE BANK
Are the bank automated transaction machines accessible?	✔	✔
Are major credit cards available?	✔	✔
Is the bank capable of international currency management?	✔	✔
Does the bank offer global investment expertise?	✘	✔
Does the bank offer stock-broker services?	✘	✔
Can income compound tax free?	✘	✔
Does the bank have strict confidentiality laws?	✘	✔
Are assets safe from third party seizure?	✘	✔

Table 3 is a list of legitimate, reputable offshore banks. We have rated them on a scale of one to five, taking into account both the bank and the country the bank is in. One star means poor, three stars mean average, and five stars mean excellent. The ratings are based on each bank's reputation, history, service levels, expertise, and perceived credit-worthiness. However, the banking world and banking laws are always changing. You should consult an offshore service provider when you set up your offshore bank account to ensure it conforms with both your local and offshore jurisdictions' reporting and tax laws, and that it is the bank best suited to your particular business and personal needs. A number of countries appearing in this table are not offshore jurisdictions, and therefore do not appear in the offshore jurisdiction reviews in Part II. However, these countries have strong banking laws useful for offshore agendas.

TABLE 3: OFFSHORE BANK RATINGS

Anguilla

Charter Bank & Trust	★★
Swiss Arab Bank & Trust	★★

Antigua and Barbuda

Antigua Commercial Bank	★★
Antigua Overseas Bank	★★
Bank of Antigua	★★
Bank of Nova Scotia	★★★
Canadian Imperial Bank of Commerce	★★★
Royal Bank of Canada (Antigua)	★★★★
Swiss American Bank	★★★

Austria

Anglo Irish Bank	★★★
Citibank (Austria)	★★★
Creditanstalt Die Bank zum Erfolg	★★

Bahamas

Bank of Montreal	★★★
Bank of New Providence	★★
Bank of Nova Scotia	★★★
Bank of the Bahamas	★★
BankAmerica Trust & Banking	★★
Barclays Bank	★★★
British American Bank	★★
Central Bank of the Bahamas	★★
Chase Manhattan Bank N.A.	★★★★
Chemical Bank & Trust (Bahamas)	★★★
Citibank N.A.	★★★
Commonwealth Bank	★★
Crédit Suisse (Bahamas)	★★★★
ENI International Bank	★★
Finance Corp. of the Bahamas	★★
First Trust Bank	★★
Gotthard Bank Nassau	★★
Handels Bank NatWest (Overseas)	★★
Handelsfinanz-C.C.F. Bank International	★★
Hang Seng (Bahamas) Bank	★★★
Hentsch Private Bank & Trust	★★
HSBC Hong Kong Bank	★★★
Laurentian Bank & Trust	★★
Lloyds Bank International (Bahamas)	★★★
National Bank of Canada (International)	★★
Royal Bank of Canada	★★★★
Royal Bank of Scotland (Nassau)	★★★★
Swiss Bank Corp. (Overseas)	★★
Westpac Bank & Trust (Bahamas)	★★★

Barbados

Bank of Nova Scotia	★★★
Barbados International Bank & Trust	★★
Barbados National Bank	★★
Barbados Savings Bank	★★
Barclays Bank PLC Offshore Banking Unit	★★★
Canadian Imperial Bank of Commerce	★★★
Central Bank of Barbados	★★★
Royal Bank of Canada	★★★★

Belize

Belize Bank (Corporate Services)	★

Bermuda

Bank of Bermuda	★★★
Bank of Butterfield Executor & Trustee	★★★
Bank of N.T. Butterfield & Son	★★
Banque SCS Alliance	★★
Bermuda Commercial Bank	★★

British Virgin Islands

Bank of East Asia	★★★★
Bank of Nova Scotia	★★★
Barclaytrust International (British Virgin Islands)	★★★

Cayman Islands

Bank of Butterfield (Cayman), Retail Banking Division	★★★
Bank of Nova Scotia	★★★
Barclays Bank	★★★
Canadian Imperial Bank of Commerce Bank & Trust	★★★
Cayman National Bank	★★★
Finsbury Bank & Trust	★★
Midland Bank Trust	★★★
Royal Bank of Canada	★★★★
Royal Trust Bank (Cayman)	★★★
Swiss Bank & Trust	★★★
Union Bank of Switzerland	★★

Cook Islands

ANZ Banking Group	★★
Westpac Banking	★★★

Gibraltar

A.L. Galliano Bankers	★★
Gibraltar Private Bank	★★
Hambros Bank (Gibraltar)	★★
Midland Bank Trust (Gibraltar)	★★★

Guernsey

ANZ Bank (Guernsey)	★★
Bank of Bermuda (Guernsey)	★★
Bank of Butterfield International (Guernsey)	★★★
Barclays Private Bank & Trust	★★★
Canadian Imperial Bank of Commerce Bank & Trust (Channel Islands)	★★★
Chemical Bank (Guernsey)	★★★
Midland Bank	★★★
Midland Bank Trustee (Guernsey)	★★

Guernsey, cont'd.

National Westminster Bank Finance ★★
Royal Bank of Canada ★★★★
Royal Bank of Scotland ★★

Hong Kong

Bank of East Asia ★★★★
Bank of N.T. Butterfield & Son ★★
Bank of Nova Scotia ★★★
Barclays Private Banking ★★★★
Chase Manhattan Private Bank ★★
Chemical Bank (Hong Kong) ★★
Coutts & Co. (Asia) ★★★★
HSBC Hong Kong Bank ★★★★
Midland Bank ★★★
Royal Trust Asia ★★
SBCI Finance Asia ★★
Standard Chartered Bank ★★
Swiss Bank ★★
Westpac Banking ★★★

Isle of Man

Anglo Manx Bank ★★★
Barclays Private Bank & Trust ★★★
Lloyds Bank ★★★
Mannin International ★★★
MeesPierson (Isle of Man) ★★
Midland Bank ★★
Midland Bank Trust (Isle of Man) ★★
Royal Bank of Scotland (Isle of Man) ★★★
Royal Trust Bank (Isle of Man) ★★
Tyndall Bank International ★★

Jersey

AIB Bank (Channel Islands) ★★
ANZ Bank (Jersey) ★★
Bank of Nova Scotia Trust Co. Channel Islands ★★★
Bank of Wales (Jersey) ★★
Barclays Private Bank & Trust ★★★
Bilbao Vizcaya Bank (Jersey) ★★
Cantrade Private Bank Switzerland (Channel Islands) ★★★
Cater Allen Bank (Jersey) ★★
Citibank (Channel Islands) ★★★
HSBC Private Banking (Channel Islands) ★★
Lloyds Bank Trust Co. (Channel Islands) ★★★
Lombard Banking (Jersey) ★★
Midland Bank ★★

Jersey, cont'd.
Midland Bank Fund Managers (Jersey) ★★
Midland Bank International Finance ★★
Royal Bank of Canada ★★★★
Royal Bank of Scotland (Jersey) ★★★
Standard Bank Investment Corp. (Jersey) ★★
Standard Chartered Bank (Channel Islands) ★★
Swiss Bank Corp. (Jersey) ★★★
TSB Bank Channel Islands ★★
TSB Bank Channel Islands Offshore Centre ★★
Westpac Banking Corp. (Jersey) ★★★

Liechtenstein
Bank of Liechtenstein ★★★
Liechtensteinische Landesbank ★★
Verwaltungs-und Privat-Bank ★★

Luxembourg
Banque de Luxembourg ★★★
Banque Générale de Luxembourg ★★
Banque Internationale à Luxembourg ★★
Chase Manhattan Bank Luxembourg ★★
Citibank (Luxembourg) ★★★
Gotthard Bank Luxembourg ★★★
G.T. Management ★★
Krediebank S.A. Luxembourgoise ★★
VP Bank (Luxembourg) ★★

Malta
Bank of Valetta International ★★
Mid-Med Bank (Overseas) ★★

Monaco
Ansbacher (Monaco) SAM ★★★★
Banque de Gotthard (Monaco) ★★
Banque de Placements et de Crédit ★★
Barclays Bank ★★★
United Overseas Bank Geneve ★★

Nauru
Bank of Nauru ★

Panama
Banco Nacional de Panamá ★
Chase Manhattan Bank N.A. ★★
Swiss Bank Corp. (Overseas) ★★

St. Kitts–Nevis
Bank of Nevis ★
Bank of Nova Scotia ★★
Barclays Bank ★★
Nevis Cooperative Banking ★
Royal Bank of Canada (St. Kitts) ★★★
St. Kitts–Nevis–Anguilla National Bank ★

Switzerland
Ansbacher (Schweiz) ★★★★
Bank Ehinger & Co. ★★★
Bank Institute Zurich ★★★
Bank J. Vontel & Co. ★★★
Banque Générale de Luxembourg (Suisse) ★★★
Barclays Bank ★★★★
Bilfinanz & Verwaltung ★★
Chase Manhattan Bank ★★★
Commercial Bank of Basel ★★
Coutts & Co. (Lausanne) ★★★★
Crédit Suisse Paradeplatz 8 ★★★
Gotthard Bank ★★★
H. Sturzeneggar & Cie ★★
Hoogwerf Trust ★★
Jyske Bank (Schweiz) ★★
Swiss Bank ★★★★
Uberseebank ★★

Turks and Caicos Islands
Bank of Nova Scotia ★★★
Barclays Bank ★★
Bordier International Bank & Trust ★★

3

OFFSHORE CORPORATE STRUCTURES

There are two primary attractions to creating an international corporate structure. First, doing so limits the liability of the individual or onshore corporation because your offshore structures are distinct legal entities from you. Once assets belong to an offshore entity, the offshore entity has legal ownership and lawsuits or creditors cannot access the offshore assets through you. (Distinct legal ownership was discussed in chapter 1, section **f.**, and you may want to refer again to Figure 1.)

Second, a foreign entity generally can hold offshore assets without incurring the high taxes and adverse risks an onshore entity might be subject to.

These two points together mean that if structured properly, the assets become the property of a foreign entity (corporation or trust) that does not have a tax or reporting requirement. The assets are no longer the legal property of the onshore individual or corporation, which does have a reporting requirement, because of the distinct legal ownership created by using offshore vehicles.

These limited liability advantages and tax advantages are available only through the offshore company, which is a

separate legal entity from its **shareholders**. Would-be creditors cannot use onshore laws to access offshore assets and cannot seek remuneration in the offshore jurisdiction (with the exception, in some jurisdictions, of remuneration required because of specific criminal actions such as money laundering, insider trading, and drug trafficking).

a. TYPES OF OFFSHORE COMPANIES

An offshore corporation is usually established in a jurisdiction that has minimal or zero taxes. In many cases, minimal taxes are accompanied by an absence of tax treaties with high-tax countries or by trade and tax treaties with high-tax countries that can create financial advantages for you or your offshore structure. Offshore companies are all allowed tax incentives and/or zero tax status depending on their resident jurisdiction's laws and treaties.

A number of different types of offshore companies are available (see section **a.2.** below). The international business company (IBC) is the most common, and it is discussed in detail here.

1. International business companies (IBCs)

The most common type of offshore company is the international business company (IBC). IBCs are ideal to use for activities such as holding assets, undertaking international business and trade, and handling investments and portfolio growth. IBCs are usually not allowed to operate in the jurisdiction in which they are registered. However, they can carry on business internationally. Business activities within the jurisdiction of residency may occur only to further the company's international activities. Usually, restrictions forbid business transactions with a resident of the jurisdiction.

IBCs are usually expected to have a registered office address, as well as a resident agent or **director**. Often, the resident agent or director is responsible for attending to the company's administrative and statutory compliance. Depending on the jurisdiction, the IBC may be suffixed with the word "Limited," "Incorporated," "Corporation," "Société Anonyme," or abbreviations of these words.

Generally, IBCs can issue most types of shares. Bearer shares are the type most commonly issued. The holder of the bearer shares is the legal owner of the company, so the certificates must be kept very securely. The holder of the bearer shares can remain anonymous and can easily transfer the shares to other shareholders. The minimum number of shareholders is usually one, and this shareholder may be an individual or a corporation of any nationality, or a trust.

Offshore jurisdictions seldom require companies to file details about the company's directors, officers, and share-holders or to file accounts of the company's financial affairs.

2. Other offshore corporate structures

Various offshore jurisdictions offer alternate forms of corporate structures. Some of these are —

- **Exempt companies**
- **Limited liability companies**
- **Limited life companies**
- Companies limited by guarantee
- Open-ended companies
- Partnerships
- Companies for public listing

These corporate structures may differ from jurisdiction to jurisdiction, and their regulations often change. Different jurisdictions have different laws, and the disadvantages or advantages of each jurisdiction depend on your specific agenda. Consult your offshore advisor for more detailed information.

b. CHOOSING AN OFFSHORE CORPORATE STRUCTURE

Because of the variety of offshore companies available in various jurisdictions, you and your financial advisor may want to consider the following issues when making your plans:

(a) Tax benefits or consequences

(b) Asset protection benefits (i.e., the amount and type of liability allowed by the company)

(c) Requirements and roles of directors

(d) Liabilities and requirements of shareholders

(e) Estate planning advantages or disadvantages

(f) Requirements for disclosure of corporate interests and activities (i.e., the amount and type of detailed reporting the law demands, or the relative privacy the law allows)

(g) Complexity of incorporation process

(h) Cost of incorporation process

(i) Requirements for and availability of company name

(j) Company constitutional requirements of memorandums and contracts

(k) Share capital requirements

(l) Public registry and dissolution requirements or constraints

(m) Management and auditing requirements and costs

(n) Foreign government controls and legal rights

c. ADVANTAGES OF OFFSHORE CORPORATE STRUCTURES

Using an offshore company has three main advantages:

(a) The absence of income taxes, corporate taxes, or **capital gains taxes** ensures that the company's assets will enjoy maximum compounded growth.

(b) Corporate privacy laws and offshore corporate structures ensure anonymity. If an offshore company is incorporated in a jurisdiction that has secrecy laws, the identity of the owner and/or **beneficiary** cannot be disclosed.

Both nominees representing the beneficial owners (the beneficiaries who will one day own the company) under a management agreement may hold shares. Also, a foreign or an onshore trust may take ownership of the shares. This is a common practice useful because it removes the ownership and control constraints from the onshore, and thus taxable, individual or corporation (trusts have different tax and reporting requirements depending on the jurisdiction they're incorporated in).

(c) An offshore company has distinct separate legal ownership of assets. This guarantees that the courts in that jurisdiction will protect these assets. Many foreign jurisdictions have advantageous asset protection, estate planning, investment, and tax laws, which help protect the offshore company's assets against attack by foreign courts.

Table 4 highlights the benefits of offshore corporations over local corporations.

Because of their flexible design, offshore companies rarely have any drawbacks for investors or business owners. Most offshore jurisdictions have structured their corporate laws to be advantageous to onshore investors and businesses. You should, however, ensure that your corporate structure has been set up properly. You must comply with the requirements of both the offshore jurisdiction and your country of residence. Be sure, also, to choose a jurisdiction that has corporate laws suitable for your financial and business needs.

TABLE 4: BENEFITS OF OFFSHORE CORPORATIONS

FEATURES	LOCAL CORPORATION	OFFSHORE CORPORATION
Is the company recognized locally and internationally?	✔	✔
Can corporate income compound tax free?	✘	✔
Are confidential directorships allowed?	✘	✔
Can directors and officers be corporations?	✘	✔
Are bearer shares allowed as a form of ownership?	✘	✔
Is the confidentiality of the shareholder ensured?	✘	✔
Can the company be exempt from holding meetings?	✘	✔

4
TRUSTS AND FOUNDATIONS

Many people would like to avoid the consequences of legal ownership of assets (e.g., taxes) while enjoying the benefits of ownership (e.g., wealth). Using trusts makes such an arrangement possible.

Most countries base their legal system on either **civil law** or **common law**. In civil law countries (such as France, Austria, and Costa Rica), domestic trusts are either uncommon or not legally recognized. This makes offshore trusts of great importance for residents of civil law countries who want to reduce their taxes and protect their assets. Common law countries (such as Canada and the United States) recognize trusts quite freely, and many people establish trusts onshore for asset protection or inheritance purposes. Offshore trusts, however, provide additional benefits. With their liberal taxation laws and strict nondisclosure arrangements, offshore jurisdictions are ideal bases for trusts of all kinds.

a. WHAT IS A TRUST?

The trust concept originated in English common law and is an equitable (or fiduciary) obligation binding the trustee to deal with the subject property under his or her control for the benefit of the beneficiaries. A trust is created when one person or entity (the **settlor**) transfers assets or property to another person or entity (the **trustee**) who then holds legal title to the transferred property in trust for the beneficiaries. The assets placed into a trust are called trust properties and may include anything that can be legally owned and transferred. Cash (bank accounts), property, and trading companies' shares are the three most common assets in offshore trusts. Other trust properties include investments (stocks and bonds), boats, cars, antiques, copyrights, land, and pension funds.

A trust can arise by operation of law or result from a verbal agreement and therefore be implied by law — your words and actions are legally acknowledged by previous, similar precedents. However, it is far more common for a trust to be explicitly established with a written document called either a deed of trust or declaration of trust. This document describes the trust and details how it is to be administered and for whose benefit.

The trustee administers the trust property for the benefit of another person (the beneficiary) and the settlor names or describes the beneficiary in the trust deed. Often a **protector** will oversee the trustee's actions. The protector may be the individual or corporation that settled the trust. The trustee can be an individual, trust company, or bank, and the settlor can also be the beneficiary.

The trustee is legally recognized as the sole owner of the trust property. The beneficiary's interest is recognized only in equity (i.e., under general principles of fairness or natural justice which supersedes the common law). This means that while the trustee has the burdens of property and ownership, the beneficiary enjoys only whatever benefits arise from the trust. These benefits may be periodic payments or terminal payments upon the trust being wound up and its assets or property distributed to the beneficiaries. However, the beneficiary does not have direct ownership of the trust property. Rather, the assets are administered by the trustee in favor of the beneficiary, who will potentially gain ownership of the assets later. A properly structured offshore trust can allow the beneficiary to receive the benefits of ownership of the assets in practice, through payments that the trustee administers, but not have legal possession, which avoids reporting or tax requirements.

You can give assets to a trust anonymously. For some people, this is one of the most valuable features of trusts. If you carefully plan your trust, you can maintain significant wealth while legally owning modest assets, because your wealth actually belongs to a trust with no legal connection to you. However, if you are doing this just for tax purposes, tax authorities tend to see through this use of trusts and tax you accordingly — in these instances it can be very hard to disprove your connection with the trust!

b. OFFSHORE TRUSTS

An offshore trust has the same structure as other trusts. A nonresident settlor creates the trust and places assets in it. The settlor can be any person or corporation, including an IBC, and the beneficiary can be any individual or company, including another IBC. In some jurisdictions you don't need to specify a beneficiary. Since most basic trusts are set up only for holding the bearer shares of the IBC, there often is no immediate need to name a beneficiary or make distributions from the trust until later.

A trustee manages the day-to-day running of the trust on behalf of the beneficiaries. The trustee is usually a licensed trust company or financial company that is resident in the trust's jurisdiction. It can also be another IBC or an individual. A trust document or deed of trust sets out specific arrangements on paper in a form that is legal in the chosen jurisdiction.

For added security, the offshore trust can be established with a letter of wishes, written by the settlor (the IBC) as a legally nonbinding guide for the trustees to follow in their management of the trust and in the distribution of the trust property. The letter should be short and to the point and can be varied or replaced by a new letter from time to time. Historically, institutional trustees have earned a reputation for adhering to the wishes of the letter. You might also appoint a protector to monitor the trustees' management of the trust if the protector is given the power to remove or replace the trustee. The protector or enforcer is usually a trusted person (often but not necessarily a nonresident) designated by the settlor to oversee the activities of the trustee. He or she acts as a safety valve to ensure that stated wishes are followed. Using either or both a letter of wishes and a protector, the settlor can maintain a degree of confidence about the administration of the trust assets.

Offshore trusts must be tailored to meet individual requirements. A typical arrangement may involve, for example, a Bahamian IBC forming a trust in the Bahamas. The IBC, not you as an individual or corporation, is the settlor of the trust because the IBC does not have any reporting requirements. If the onshore individual or corporation were the settlor, an onshore tax authority could claim tax and reporting requirements.

Because the IBC settles the trust, the IBC is solidified as a separate, distinct entity from the onshore individual or corporation (see Figure 2). Because the trust owns the IBC, assets will flow first into the company, where they can remain or be transferred up to the trust for further accumulation or distribution to the beneficiaries. The legal ownership of the IBC is held in the trust separate and distinct from any onshore individual or corporation. This arrangement adds a double layer of confidentiality to the trust and offers both privacy advantages and tax advantages. The IBC and the trust are themselves two separate elements which together offer greater flexibility and many benefits. The IBC adds further greater flexibility since it can also be transferred to another jurisdiction if needed.

c. TYPES OF OFFSHORE TRUSTS

Trusts may be established for many purposes. Some of the more common types of trusts follow.

1. Beneficial trusts

A beneficial trust is a popular type of trust, largely because of its simplicity. In a beneficial trust, the trust document identifies the beneficiaries and specifies that they are the ultimate owners of the assets upon distribution of any income resulting from the trust. For example, the trust document might read "Jill Doe will receive the sum of $100,000 on her 25th birthday." Because beneficiaries are specifically named, beneficial trusts can be valuable for asset protection and inheritance tax planning. However, they are not considered valuable for other types of tax planning or maintaining

FIGURE 2: THE ASSETS FLOW INTO THE COMPANY

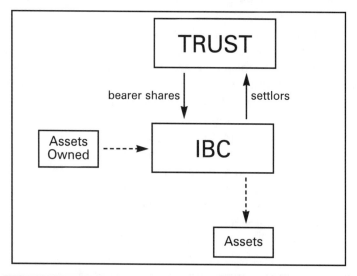

privacy, as the IRS or Revenue Canada will inevitably have claim to a taxpayer's income and have rights, through reporting rules, to be informed of the trust's existence.

The assets may become taxable if the beneficiary is an onshore entity and is also the settlor. Under these circumstances, the IRS and Revenue Canada may assess that the beneficiary is the owner of the assets and thus taxable, even if the income is not received.

2. Discretionary trusts

Discretionary trusts are those in which the interests of the beneficiaries are not fixed, leaving the trustee with the discretion to determine how, when, to whom, and in what proportion to distribute trust assets. Discretionary trusts allow the trustees to describe the beneficiaries by class rather than name them in a trust document. Since no specific beneficiaries are named in the trust document, revenue authorities cannot tax any potential beneficiaries — there is no way of knowing when, or even if, they will benefit from the trust, although (in theory) tax is payable on the receipt of the proceeds of the trust by a specific beneficiary. By properly establishing the trust, a beneficiary can avoid excessive taxes.

A discretionary trust requires that you have a high level of confidence in your selected trustee. The trustee could potentially name beneficiaries as he or she sees fit. There are, however, a number of safeguards against this. Trustees worldwide will generally observe the following rules:

(a) In many offshore jurisdictions, local governments require that trustees obtain a license. Governments are interested in maintaining exemplary relations with offshore clients, and so the licensing process is strictly controlled and the trustee must have a proven, reputable history. If a trustee engages in misconduct, the license is immediately withdrawn.

(b) The settlor can write a letter of wishes, setting out specific requests for management and distribution of the assets of the offshore trust. The settlor can alter the contents of this letter at any time. The trustee uses this letter as a guiding principle, but it is not legally binding. It does, however, allow the settlor to have some say in controlling the trust, while not creating a reporting or tax obligation.

(c) The settlor can appoint a protector or guardian who observes the management and distribution of the assets and retains control over the trustee. Individuals and corporations frequently use discretionary trusts to hold assets, directly or indirectly, through offshore companies. The offshore company acquires assets (such as real estate, marketable securities, or pleasure yachts). But the trust owns all the shares in the company, which encompasses the assets the company acquires. If the offshore vehicle is properly structured, you can exercise a great degree of certainty over the administration of the assets without having the tax and reporting burdens that legal ownership brings. Because the trust puts extra distance between you and the assets, it is recommended that you use a trust in conjunction with an offshore company. In this way, you can enjoy the following benefits:

- The shares in the company are held offshore where privacy, confidentiality, and tax minimization are available.
- The trust can hold a number of companies which trade around the world. It is often complicated to bring a group of companies together in any productive manner unless a discretionary trust owns the shares of the companies.

3. Revocable trusts

Revocable trusts enable the settlor to voluntarily transfer title to his or her assets, with certain conditions attached to this transfer. A wide variety of real, personal, or mixed assets can be held in a revocable trust, including money, insurance policies, homes, cars, boats, shares of stock, or ownership of a corporation. There is usually one trustee who holds title to the assets, but more trustees can be named to manage the affairs of the transferred property.

A revocable trust allows the settlor to dictate the trust terms, withdraw assets, and dissolve the trust by formal revocation so that the trust assets revert to the settlor. This type of trust, however, has its shortcomings in terms of asset protection and tax liability. If the settlor is also the beneficiary, revocable trusts are relatively easy targets for creditors during the settlor's lifetime (even though accessing the offshore assets is a complex procedure). When the settlor dies, the revocable trust becomes irrevocable and is administered by a trustee for the benefit of named beneficiaries.

4. Asset protection trusts

Asset protection trusts provide protection for the settlor and the beneficiaries from all forms of claims that may be made against them. Used as early as the Middle Ages, they have evolved to protect assets against risks ranging from political unrest to investment or matrimonial concerns.

On their own, asset protection trusts cannot offer tax reduction. But in combination with an offshore company, they can provide valuable tax reductions. They are ideal for people whose lifestyle or profession may leave them open to either legal or civil claims, and are popular in the United States (where more than 90% of the world's civil suits originate). Many doctors and surgeons use offshore asset protection trusts to avoid exposure to malpractice suits. These trusts are also used to protect personal and family assets against claims by partners in matrimonial divorce cases. Business owners and partners can use these trusts to protect themselves against the financial consequences of a legal claim against them personally following a claim on their business.

By setting up asset protection trusts offshore, you will find several additional benefits that are not available from domestic asset protection trusts. Similar vehicles such as family limited partnerships and limited liability companies are becoming increasingly vulnerable to creditors. In contrast, a correctly established offshore trust has yet to be dismantled by a domestic court (except in criminal cases).

Some offshore jurisdictions have introduced legislation that resolves the problems and concerns arising from domestic asset protection trusts. The new trust legislation is designed to protect trusts against future creditors and places the burden of proof with the creditors. The assets in the trust are protected by law as long as the events giving rise to the lawsuit occurred after the trust was formed. For example, legal proceedings are launched against a settlor in his or her resident jurisdiction. However, the settlor established a trust before the events that led to the lawsuit, so the assets in the trust are safe. A judgment in any court against the settlor is not enforceable against an offshore trustee because the settlor and the trustee are legally distinct. The creditor must begin independent proceedings in the offshore jurisdiction's courts — a very expensive and time-consuming procedure with little chance of success.

Assets will be protected further if the settlor is not also the trustee or if the settlor is a foreign corporation. Neither the settlor nor the onshore corporation or individual should be the direct or sole beneficiary, as this may leave such a settlor with a tax burden. You should also be sure to define and limit the powers of the protector if he or she is also the settlor.

An asset protection trust set up specifically to defraud or avoid legal proceedings is invalidated by a number of trust laws. These laws also designate a time limit of generally two years in which a creditor can challenge the trust, after which time the assets are safe. The offshore asset protection trust is a planning tool designed to protect you not against possible creditors of whom you are aware but from future illegitimate claimants and possible financial disaster.

d. ADVANTAGES OF OFFSHORE TRUSTS

When implemented and maintained effectively, offshore trusts can provide protection against:

- income tax, probate fees, and capital gains tax in Canada;
- gift or estate duties in the United States;
- bankruptcy and creditors;
- spousal support and maintenance claims; and
- lawsuits for negligence and claims for damages.

A properly structured offshore trust will provide better protection than an onshore trust. In most circumstances, you will not need to pay any additional income taxes or gift or estate duties.

In addition, an offshore trust can offer the following benefits:

- security to accumulate and preserve assets,
- reduction of risk and liability,
- privacy and confidentiality in personal and business affairs,
- flexibility to adjust to changing economic and legal situations,
- asset management in the event of disability or death,
- minimization of **estate taxes** and elimination of the delay and costs of **probate**,
- financial control over capital and assets and financial mobility, and
- freedom to distribute your wealth as you choose.

Table 5 outlines some of the advantages offshore trusts have over local trusts. Some offshore jurisdictions (e.g., the

Bahamas, Liechtenstein, the Cook Islands, and the Cayman Islands) have made specific efforts to promote themselves as good locations for trust formation. Their legislation includes provisions that specifically facilitate the protection of wealth, such as:

- Protection from spendthrift beneficiaries: beneficiaries cannot draw extravagant income from the trust, and deplete the wealth of assets.
- Avoidance of heirship rules: you can name anyone as the successor to your wealth.
- Elimination of rules against perpetuities or accumulative restrictions: thus, funds can be added to the trust and the trust can be formed for much longer durations.
- Nonenforcement of foreign judgments under any circumstances: judgments made in other jurisdictions' courts will not have any effect in your offshore jurisdiction. Would-be creditors must pursue their claims in offshore courts as well, which is costly and time-consuming, and with little chance of success.

TABLE 5: COMPARISON OF LOCAL AND OFFSHORE TRUSTS

FEATURES	LOCAL TRUST	OFFSHORE TRUST
Is the trust recognized locally and internationally?	✔	✔
Does the trust provide for asset protection?	✘	✔
Can the trust be maintained perpetually?	✘	✔
Can the trust be transferred to another jurisdiction?	✘	✔
Can trust income compound tax free?	✘	✔
Does the trust provide confidentiality?	✘	✔

e. MAINTAINING OFFSHORE TRUST SECURITY

In most offshore jurisdictions, offshore trusts are reputable and highly regulated. Although fraud by licensed or unlicensed trustees is virtually nonexistent, well-developed controls and laws are nevertheless firmly in place.

A good way for the settlor to prevent fraud is to appoint a protector. The protector regularly, and on demand, receives pertinent information on the status, records, and accounts of the trust. It is possible to also word the deed of trust to provide for the instant dismissal and replacement of trustees.

To maintain complete control over the trust if tax issues are not relevant, the settlor can also act as his or her own trustee through an enduring **power of attorney**. However, the legal status in some jurisdictions of this situation is not always certain and it is not advisable.

f. SETTING UP AN OFFSHORE TRUST

Once you have decided to set up an offshore trust, you need to pick a jurisdiction, appoint trustees, and decide who will write and execute the deed of trust. Many people erringly believe that trust setup and maintenance are costly. This belief is sometimes fueled by advisors who justify their high fees by the fact that trusts generally contain significant holdings — they set their fees based on assumptions of what you can afford. It's a good idea to discuss fees with your advisor at the outset of your planning.

It is important to choose a jurisdiction that is recognized internationally to ensure that the validity of your trust will be enforced. The jurisdiction you choose should have good trust laws and meet your particular criteria (e.g., it has strong bank secrecy or an extensive treaty network). Your trust must comply with the offshore jurisdiction's laws. It is best to consult both an offshore professional and someone who is knowledgeable about the laws and legal precedents of your onshore jurisdiction.

Asking the right questions now can save you major difficulties later on. Some questions to consider are —

- *Where is the offshore jurisdiction in relation to my home country?*
  Many people decide to locate their trusts in an offshore jurisdiction that is geographically removed from them, thus creating a physical and psychological barrier between the laws of their home country and their assets. On the other hand, some trust holders like to know their holdings are geographically close by.

- *To what extent is my privacy and confidentiality assured?*
  In some offshore jurisdictions, it is possible to rely so heavily on the privacy of financial holdings that if faced with claims at home, confidence can be had that the offshore assets are safe.

- *Can I move my trust to another jurisdiction?*
  It is highly unlikely that you will ever need to move your trust to another jurisdiction, but it may be necessary in extreme cases. Generally, trust laws are similar throughout many offshore jurisdictions, so trusts can be mobile. In some instances, moving your trust is encouraged. For example, a government is elected in your offshore jurisdiction that stated in its electoral platform that it would willingly share information with other jurisdictions, if asked. To avoid compromising your financial privacy, you could easily move your offshore trust.

Each jurisdiction has specific legal issues you will need to consider. One such issue involves the extent of a jurisdiction's authority. For example, if an offshore jurisdiction is a signatory to the **Hague Convention**, it may be required or pressured to recognize judgments from foreign courts.

g. OFFSHORE FOUNDATIONS

A private **foundation** acts like a trust and operates like a company. A foundation consists of three groups of people: founders, beneficiaries, and the foundation council.

The founders are the people or corporate entities that establish the foundation by endowing it with liquid or property assets. A liquid asset is something that you can easily convert into cash, like a bank account or a bond. An example of a property asset is real estate or a boat.

The foundation regulations will specify beneficiaries. Beneficiaries' names are kept in the strictest privacy at the registered office in the jurisdiction where the foundation is established.

The foundation council can be made up of individuals or their legal counsel. The foundation council is responsible for managing assets, carrying on business, informing the beneficiaries of the economic status of the foundation, allocating assets to the beneficiaries, and taking care of the foundation's legalities as set out in the laws for private foundations. Offshore service providers are often able to provide members for the foundation council if asked. The foundation also requires a resident agent, who must be either a lawyer or a law firm.

The foundation becomes a corporate body by registering a foundation charter at the public registry. Even though the foundation is registered, you can still enjoy secrecy and anonymity. It is very simple to administer the foundation with complete management privacy. There is no need to indicate beneficiaries, and the filing requirements for annual returns or financial statements are minimal. An offshore foundation is exempt from all taxes.

Legally, the foundation assets are entirely separate from the founder's personal assets. The founder's creditors have the right to object to the founder's contribution or transfer of assets to the foundation if the contribution constitutes a fraudulent act against the creditors or if the contribution occurs fewer than three years before the creditor's complaint.

You can establish a proper offshore foundation only in Panama, Liechtenstein, and Austria. However, only Panama and Liechtenstein offer foundation law that is suitable for North American offshore purposes.

5
FORMING AND OWNING
AN OFFSHORE BANK

a. WHAT IS AN OFFSHORE BANK?

Some individuals and corporations are not content with just an offshore bank account but want more control over their money while offshore. Purchasing or forming a private offshore bank is one option available to them.

Offshore banks are banks in jurisdictions that allow strict banking secrecy. They have the same or similar responsibilities as local banks and, in some cases, are more strictly controlled. Often, offshore banks don't have the reporting, disclosure, or regulatory requirements that are common onshore, but they have well-developed guidelines and responsibilities that they must adhere to and respect. They are also responsible to, and obliged to disclose information to, the central bank of their jurisdiction.

A bank can be formed in almost any country in the world. Offshore banks are typically formed in the Bahamas, the British Virgin Islands, the Cayman Islands, and Cyprus. It is also relatively inexpensive and simple to form a bank in Belize, Mauritius, Nevis, Panama, and Vanuatu.

b. WHO SHOULD CONSIDER FORMING AN OFFSHORE BANK?

Forming an offshore bank is not for everyone. Setting one up can often be complicated, depending on the class, restriction, and purpose of the bank. Offshore banks can be small and simple, owned by one person for a specific purpose, or they can be large corporations, like the Royal Bank of Canada. In some jurisdictions, incorporating a bank can be as simple as forming an IBC. However, if it's that easy, the jurisdiction is probably not recognized as a legitimate banking center.

Bear in mind that when you form an offshore bank, you get what you pay for. There are jurisdictions where you can form a bank for as little as $25,000. However, if this is done incorrectly or if your intentions are not legitimate, your bank could be little more than a $25,000 piece of paper! As well, many onshore banks will not recognize private offshore banks that are clearly set up for a single purpose (such as tax reduction or investment).

Individuals or corporations with an international agenda should consider forming an offshore bank if they are —

- Venture capitalists
- Investment management companies
- Project management companies
- Estate management companies
- Entities seeking hedging strategies
- Entities with a large portfolio of investments

You should also consider forming an offshore bank if you need —

- the ability to be a third party to a transaction,
- a customized letter of credit, or
- more banking flexibility than a traditional banking service can offer in order to meet the demands of your specific agenda.

c. TYPES OF OFFSHORE BANKS

There are three categories or classes of offshore banks:
(a) class A unrestricted,
(b) class B unrestricted, and
(c) class B restricted, also called class C.

An offshore bank must adhere to the banking laws of its resident jurisdiction. These laws are different in each area, but they generally specify that a bank must have a minimum number of employees; it must have a minimum **capitalization** (the initial funds or capital establishing the bank), or minimum deposits held with the central bank of that jurisdiction; and, in most cases, the owners of the bank must have relevant banking experience. In order to operate the bank outside of the jurisdiction in which it is incorporated, the bank must also meet the regulatory approval of the second jurisdiction (e.g., Canada, Britain, or the United States).

1. Class A unrestricted

Major local banks such as Citibank, Barclays, and Royal Bank of Canada are examples of Class A unrestricted banks. They offer all services, including retail and walk-in banking services, and are allowed to do banking business with locals in their own jurisdiction. However, these offshore banks can provide more services than can similar onshore banks. Many are insured, but not all are. Class A offshore banks are often more aggressive than onshore banks and market their services internationally. Class A unrestricted banks are very difficult to set up. Usually only existing world-class international banks will qualify to form a class A unrestricted bank or be permitted to set up in an offshore jurisdiction.

2. Class B unrestricted

Class B unrestricted banks operate like class A unrestricted banks, except that they cannot do walk-in trade. Most private commercial banks offshore are class B unrestricted banks. They are also quite difficult to set up. The **principals** must have extensive banking history and the capitalization must be at least $2 million. Most international banks set up offshore class B unrestricted banks, as local walk-in retail banking does not account for a large percentage of international business.

3. Class B restricted (or class C)

Class B restricted banks are subject to the same limitations as class B unrestricted banks. An additional limit sets the maximum number of clients a class B restricted bank is allowed, usually about ten. These banks can easily meet most banking needs such as obtaining letters of credit and accessing loans or investments. However, most of these banks cannot issue checks, money orders, or bank drafts. Banking is usually done by wire. In many cases, a class B restricted bank will be set up for only one significant project. Such banks are by far the most common type of bank formed offshore, because the cost to set one up is relatively inexpensive (approximately $100,000, which includes capitalization). The principals do not need previous banking experience.

d. FORMING YOUR OFFSHORE BANK

Because of the strict rules involved in international banking, it is crucial that you structure your bank properly. The resolutions, infrastructures, and charters should reflect the principals' agenda and should comply with the jurisdiction's requirements.

You can either buy or create your own bank. There are two advantages to buying an existing bank. First, the bank has an established (and hopefully reputable) history and operation and is therefore credible in the eyes of clients and the authorities. Second, obtaining the relevant approvals for your bank can be a costly and time-consuming procedure. An established bank already has these approvals. It is often faster and more cost-effective to simply acquire an offshore bank rather than create your own.

If you are considering forming or purchasing an offshore bank in order to reduce your taxes in either the United States or Canada, you must ensure that your government considers your structure nontaxable. This often means forming a bank in a reputable banking jurisdiction and ensuring that the parties involved — either as lenders, debtors, or in the business associated with the bank — are independent parties.

6
GLOBAL INVESTING

Many of the fastest growing markets in the world — the ones that have delivered the highest returns to their investors over the past ten years — are outside North America. Emerging markets, including the Pacific Rim, Latin America, and China, offer strong long-term opportunities because of their high growth potential and gradual shift toward free-market policies (in a free market, prices are determined by competition, not legislation).

Today, a global economy is emerging. Countries around the world are opening their capital markets to global investors, reducing the rate of government spending and borrowing, and privatizing government-controlled enterprises. They must continue to evolve to remain competitive in an increasingly efficient, technologically sophisticated, and free-trade oriented global economy.

Since an increasing number of profitable opportunities originate overseas, many investors choose to establish a confidential offshore brokerage account and seek out a competent investment manager who can advise them on global investment opportunities. When you consider offshore investing (instead of limiting yourself to onshore), investment options multiply immediately.

The Standard and Poors 500 Index is an indicator of U.S. stocks and is a compilation of 500 large-, medium-, and small-sized companies. Investors generally consider that the Standard and Poors Index is a leader (a precursor) to most other major world stock markets. On days when the closing value of the Standard and Poors Index has increased, generally other major world markets increase in the following trading session. Although the Standard and Poors 500 Index increased by 30% in 1997, foreign markets were far more profitable. Germany was up 48%, Italy 48%, Switzerland 50%, Venezuela 50%, Hungary 53%, Mexico 60%, Greece 68%, and Brazil 70% (i.e., the value of the index increased by the corresponding percentage).

Many investors do not take advantage of offshore opportunities because of the myth that offshore investing is illegal. However, when you structure your offshore project properly, you can legally invest globally and —

(a) transfer your domestic funds to low-tax or no-tax jurisdictions,

(b) transfer funds confidentially,

(c) use offshore vehicles to invest outside the offshore jurisdiction,

(d) pay little or no tax, and let investments grow while accumulating compound interest,

(e) avoid reporting requirements on the initial transfers and the investment assets, and

(f) reduce tax liability on the investment's growth.

a. WHAT IS INVESTING?

Investing is a process in which an investor commits some of his or her funds to a project or company with the expectation of earning a future financial return. An investment can refer to either the money invested itself (such as a check you write or shares you buy), or to a process called "leveraging" a property or asset, which means using the property or asset as collateral for an investment. Most individuals will make investments in cash, but some corporations may finance investments with assets instead.

You might invest in a company, mutual fund, or other entity by buying shares, which are units of ownership of that entity. You can invest in publicly accessible entities, such as stocks trading on the stock market or bonds a government sells. You can also use private investments, such as investing in a closely held company or investing in an entity that only certain people can access. Public investments (like the stock market) are easier to convert into cash than private investments.

A group of investments is called a portfolio. A portfolio can contain different kinds of investment products. Most investors design their portfolio with a particular focus, such as aggressive growth, conservative growth, or wealth preservation, based on their needs and future desires. You can change the focus of your portfolio by adding to or subtracting from the investments you hold in it. Changing the percentage of stocks, bonds, mutual funds, or other investment products in your portfolio will determine the portfolio's rates of overall risk and return. The ratio between risk and return is called the investment's "beta," and a low beta means a low risk level for a given return.

When you are choosing an offshore jurisdiction in which to hold your investments, you might consider the jurisdiction's reputation and political stability, the presence of suitable investment firms you can invest through, access to foreign markets, and your ability to communicate easily with your investment advisors (so that you will know what is happening with your foreign investments).

Using your offshore investments to access foreign markets can be as simple as choosing foreign investment products (stocks, bonds, and mutual funds) to hold in your portfolio. A foreign investment product is any investment

outside your home country. You can use foreign investments to effectively increase your returns by reducing
the applicable taxes you pay on your investments as well as
reducing your portfolio's overall risk by increasing diversification. Holding foreign investments also lets you
capitalize on the growth of foreign markets and reduce the
risks of holding all your investments in one country. You
can hold these investments in different currencies, which
can lessen the impact of sudden currency changes. The
advantages of using foreign investments are discussed in
more detail in section **c.** below.

b. TYPES OF INVESTMENT PRODUCTS

Investors around the world can choose from a variety of
investment products. Each has a different potential risk and
return. Some common types of investment products are —
(a) Stocks
(b) Bonds
(c) Mutual funds
(d) Derivatives
(e) Private investments

Many other investment products are available, and institutions are constantly inventing new combinations of
investment products. Generally, these five classes are the
main kinds of investments.

1. Stocks

Stocks, also commonly referred to as equities, securities,
and shares, are units of ownership in a company. Stocks
come in two forms: common shares, which represent the
true growth of the company and carry voting rights, and
preferred shares, which represent the ongoing income and
profit of the underlying company. You can purchase stocks
either on a stock market, if it is a public company, or privately if a private company is doing a private placement

(i.e., selling an investment product privately, not publicly on the stock exchange)or seed financing (getting the initial capital to start a company).

2. Bonds

While stocks represent ownership in the underlying company or organization, bonds represent that underlying company's financial commitment (debt) to the holder — bonds are a debt instrument. Other kinds of debt instruments are T-bills (treasury bills, or debt issued by the treasury) and government bonds. Government bonds are usually less risky (i.e., less chance of default) than corporate bonds. As well, bonds are usually less risky than stocks, but bond risk fluctuates depending on the type and the status of the underlying company or government issuer.

Typically, bonds have specific purchase values and interest rates. For example, bonds may sell only in denominations of $100 or $500, meaning you could not buy a bond for $275. Similarly, the interest rate might be set to a particular rate, regardless of how interest rates change in other markets or over the time you hold the bond.

3. Mutual funds

Mutual funds are a collection of investment products that are mutually owned by a number of investors. The type and number of products in the fund will vary depending on the fund's objectives and risk tolerance. Investors purchase units in the fund which entitle them to the return (or loss, if any) the fund receives. Most mutual fund companies take a management fee for administering the fund, but most investors are happy to pay a fee in exchange for a diversified portfolio, professional management, and peace of mind in knowing that their money is to some extent safe under the fund's management. In recent years, most mutual funds have not outperformed the indexes (or markets) in which they invest.

4. Derivatives

Derivative products include more sophisticated investments than stocks or bonds, such as options, futures, and investable indexes. Options let the investor buy or sell the investment at a set price on or before a certain date. He or she has the option to take advantage of this, but does not have to. Futures refer to any investment that require the seller to deliver a return or asset in the future. An investable index, such as the Standard and Poors Index, is a collection of many stocks. If you invest in the index, your returns are based on the overall performance of all the stocks in the index.

Options, futures, investable indexes, and other derivative products are more volatile than the underlying companies or stocks associated with them, or than other investment products. Some investors find this volatility attractive because they can potentially enjoy significant returns very quickly. However, these same products can also suffer huge losses just as rapidly.

Sophisticated investors can successfully use derivative products to hedge (reduce the risk) other investments. Some active traders deal exclusively in derivative products.

5. Private investments

Many investment houses and brokerage firms as well as private companies will offer private investment opportunities into investment products that may not be as liquidable (not as easy to buy and sell out of) as public investment options but may have merit depending on the specific investor's objectives and portfolio. Many times, these private investments can have very significant returns if the project is successful or if the private company later goes to a public offering. These types of investments commonly fall into categories such as financing a new company (seed financing), real estate investments, or the financing of a new or special project.

c. OFFSHORE ADVANTAGES

1. Global diversity

The U.S. stock markets offer a wide variety of investment options to choose from, and the Canadian stock markets, while smaller, also have attractive investment options. When you invest with a domestic focus, you limit your investment selection. Many domestic institutions restrict the level of foreign-content investments they accept. This leads to limited competition: in a domestic environment, only domestic financial institutions compete for your investment dollars.

If you want to invest in the world's top five companies in sectors such as banking, housing, chemicals, automobiles, engineering, or construction, for example, you must look internationally. When you turn to offshore, your investment options expand. Jurisdictions and financial institutions compete for your investment dollars on a global scale. Increased competition means improved returns for the investor — you.

2. Risks decrease and returns increase

Investment options must offer high returns at an acceptable level of risk for investors to find them attractive. Offshore investment institutions' low reporting and infrastructure costs allow them to offer better returns than onshore investment institutions while maintaining acceptable risk levels. Because of this, the rate of return is generally considered to be 2% higher on average offshore for the same level of risk onshore. As your investment compounds tax-free over several years, your portfolio can become much larger than its onshore counterpart.

Whenever you invest, whether you focus onshore or off-shore, it is impossible to eliminate all risk. However, you can diminish the effects of international investment risks.

Several studies have shown that a globally diversified portfolio of international securities has a lower overall risk level than a portfolio of investments limited to U.S. or Canadian equities. Global diversification, simultaneous exposure to different countries and industries, and a long-term perspective can help reduce the effects of these risks. Foreign markets can, and do, move independently of U.S. and Canadian markets, and of each other — that is why an offshore-based investment can help decrease the volatility of your overall investment returns. Whether you focus on currency diversification, better product selection, or international competition, offshore investments offer a better risk/return ratio.

Figure 3 illustrates how risks can decrease and returns can increase when you add global investments to your portfolio. In this figure, an equity portfolio with a 50% global and 50% domestic investment would have produced a lower risk factor and a higher return over a ten-year period than an all-domestic portfolio.

FIGURE 3: THEORY OF DIVERSIFICATION

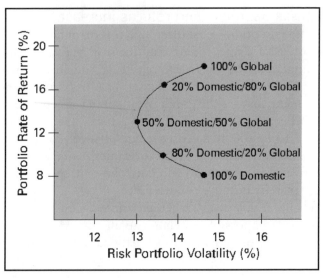

3. Global means growth

Offshore investing is concerned primarily with growth, not income. Any income your investments earn is rolled back into the investment so it can grow more. This way, any taxes (such as withholding taxes) are effectively discounted. For example, if you were an offshore investor who bought a U.S. equity with a 10% dividend, 30% of this dividend would be withheld at the source. You would end up not with 10% of the value of the equity as income, but only 7%. This would not happen in good offshore investment jurisdictions.

Global diversity and reduced risk work hand in hand. The more diverse your portfolio is, the more your risk is spread out and volatility minimized, and the more your investments can grow. Poor performance in one market may be offset by superior performance in another market. In addition, there are now great opportunities in emerging markets. The economic restructuring occurring outside North America is creating excellent opportunities for profitable investing. Returns obtained offshore can substantially exceed the returns achieved through domestic investments with equivalent risk.

Figure 4 demonstrates how tax-free offshore investments, when compounded over 12 years, can yield a return almost twice as much as onshore investments.

d. TAKING THE FIRST STEP

If you have never invested offshore before, there are four things to bear in mind when developing a global portfolio —

(a) Don't think of offshore investing as an alternative to domestic investing. Instead, global investing should be seen as a way to achieve greater diversification, both geographically and in product and selection, and to decrease risk and increase your returns. In many ways, it should be seen as an extension to your current portfolio.

(b) Pay attention to your comfort level. If you haven't previously invested offshore, start with a small portfolio, perhaps a managed account. When you feel comfortable, increase your holdings offshore. Test the waters, then move your investments as appropriate.

(c) If you don't have a lot of investing experience, find and use a knowledgeable investment management firm or portfolio manager. The presence of offshore structures does not stop investment advisors from being involved — they simply administer the process through different means. Like any investments, your global investments have to be seen in the context of your whole investment portfolio. You'll want to think about how these investments fit in with your overall financial plan, your risk tolerance, and your comfort level.

(d) Give your investments time to produce results. Many overseas markets, especially some of the emerging markets, have been experiencing rapid growth. However, as these economies and their businesses make their own adjustments to global competition, they have also experienced large and rapid declines in price.

FIGURE 4: COMPARISON OF ONSHORE AND OFFSHORE INVESTMENT RETURNS

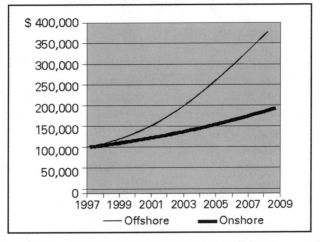

7
ASSET PROTECTION AND ESTATE PLANNING

Over 40 million civil lawsuits are filed each year in North America, and a significant proportion of them are petty, unsubstantiated cases. Today's civil court cases have more to do with who has unprotected assets that can be attacked than they do with actual negligence or harm. Frivolous or not, they generate substantial costs and the verdicts can demand substantial awards. Individuals and corporations owe it to themselves, their shareholders, and their families to protect their assets and avoid unnecessary losses.

a. THE PROTECTION OF WEALTH

This century has provided unlimited opportunities for wealth creation, particularly in Canada and the United States. In many instances that wealth is now passing on as inheritances. Without appropriate asset protection, much of that wealth can be lost through the failure of benefactors and their advisors to take the appropriate steps to protect their asset base.

For people who have accumulated personal or business wealth, protecting that wealth has become an essential concern. Many individuals and corporations in high-tax jurisdictions use financial planning to minimize income taxes, gift taxes, or estate taxes. You can use business or investment structures to take advantage of offshore exemptions or of concessions available under your home country's tax legislation.

Until recently, few people gave serious attention to protecting their wealth from risks such as creditors and lawsuits. Today, no financial planning strategy is complete unless you review the overall risk profile and consider asset protection.

b. ASSET PROTECTION PLANNING

Much of the financial planning in Canada and the United States uses domestic (onshore) financial services that include estate planning arrangements and encompass relatively new concepts such as limited liability companies, family limited partnerships, and asset protection trusts. However, offshore-based trusts used for domestic asset protection strategies are emerging as a primary component of such planning.

Before you arrange your offshore asset protection, it's important that you understand domestic law. You should be familiar with the laws governing estate duties or inheritance taxes, capital gains taxes, income tax, and bankruptcy. In particular, you should know the difference between transferring asset ownership legitimately or fraudulently, and you should know how marriage settlements, and currency or foreign investment controls, may affect you. This information will help you decide if it's feasible for you to establish an offshore-based asset protection structure and what kind of assets you should transfer. An offshore professional should be able to advise you. Costs of asset protection planning may vary greatly, depending on the scope of risks, complexity of assets, and specific agendas.

c. ASSET PROTECTION AND FINANCIAL PRIVACY

Investing offshore can effectively protect your assets from potential risks and keep your financial affairs private. In North America today, anyone can obtain information about your private affairs for as little as $100, through, for example your social insurance or social security number, a credit check, credit card databases, or public registry office. This personal information might include:

- where you bank,
- the value of your business assets,
- which brokerage accounts you have,
- how many houses you own and what they are worth,
- what your buying habits are,
- what your annual income is,
- what property taxes you pay, and
- your medical history.

A properly set up offshore structure restricts access to this information. Those who want information about your offshore interests must go to extraordinary lengths to get it. Most often they must appeal to a foreign court (a costly and time-consuming task) before they can hope even to interview your financial manager or banker. In many jurisdictions, unless under a local court order, financial and banking managers can be imprisoned for even divulging a client's name!

d. BENEFITS OF ASSET PROTECTION

1. Increase your financial privacy

Asset protection generally involves transferring your assets into a variety of foreign legal business structures that are less visible and accessible to others than are domestic business structures. This decreased visibility offers you financial privacy. Using these structures, you can also reduce the amount of your personal assets or income, which may discourage other people from suing you.

2. Avoid future lawsuits

The most effective way to avoid a lawsuit is to be "judgment-proof," meaning that the courts cannot affect you. Asset protection won't make you judgment-proof, but it can help you discourage lawsuits. Your offshore structure can reduce the likelihood that someone could seize your assets. Once you transfer assets, you no longer have legal ownership of them. Asset protection can also replace liability insurance (see section **d.4.** below). If you have few or no assets or insurance, it's less likely that others will take you to court over petty, unsubstantiated things — you aren't an attractive target.

3. Negotiate favorable court settlements

If you lose a lawsuit but your assets are held offshore, it's extremely difficult for the plaintiff to get the full settlement of the judgment. You will often be able to negotiate a settlement for 20% to 50% of the judgment.

4. Save on liability insurance costs

For risk management, asset protection can be an effective alternative to liability insurance. Professionals and business owners can reduce excessive insurance costs. Often, getting insurance for the full amount you might potentially be sued for is very expensive. You might theoretically be sued for $5 million, but you are only insured for $2 million — more insurance is cost prohibitive. In these situations, asset protection is an excellent option. When some of your assets are owned offshore, your offshore assets are safe from any lawsuits you might face, no matter how much you are sued for. With a well-developed asset protection plan, you can gradually reduce how much insurance coverage you require. Substantial reductions in insurance premiums will offset the cost of asset protection.

5. Take advantage of favorable offshore laws

In some jurisdictions, trust and estate laws favor the defendant over the creditor. This is another way offshore asset protection can help make you a less likely target for creditors. When you are choosing a location for your offshore needs, find out if and how the jurisdiction's laws favor the defendant. This is one of the most important things to consider in planning offshore asset protection.

The Bahamas, the Cook Islands, and Luxembourg are considered to have the best trust laws for asset protection. In these jurisdictions, a creditor in your home country has to sue the trustee of the foreign trust, in the foreign courts, based on the laws of the foreign jurisdiction. This is a costly, time-consuming, and often unsuccessful process.

A number of offshore jurisdictions impose time limits on legal claims. For example, if the trust is set up two years (or a similar term) before a legal claim is made, the assets in the trust are safe. The only exception to this is if there is criminal activity or if a domestic creditor can prove, based on the laws of the foreign country, within their **statute of limitations**, that you fraudulently transferred property or other assets to the trust.

6. Avoid excessive legal fees

In countries with laws that favor the defendant, the defendant cannot be charged legal fees because he or she is innocent until proven guilty. To pursue the case, the plaintiff will have to pay the legal fees for both sides. The plaintiff must also pay any travel expenses for witnesses and/or domestic lawyers pursuing the case in the foreign jurisdiction.

7. Avoid probate and estate taxes

Probate is the process of validating a will. The fees charged are based on the value of the estate assets. Although you can avoid probate by using a revocable domestic trust, it is far more cost-effective to use an offshore trust. An offshore trust is less expensive, and it offers additional asset protection advantages. Section **f.1.** discusses this in more detail.

8. Enjoy trust mobility

When you draft the structure of your offshore trust, you can provide for a situation where the protector (or the trustee) can move the trust to another jurisdiction. This is useful if there is any chance that the first jurisdiction might become "risky" for the trust — for example, its political situation might change. This feature can also increase a creditor's costs and time in getting an attachment, the legal document that authorizes the court to take custody of your trust assets. The added costs and time reduce the likelihood that creditors will attack your assets in the first place.

9. Retain control over the assets

Some people find it difficult or unacceptable to give up direct control over their property — they would rather take their chances on being sued. So that settlors can retain control over their assets, some asset protection experts (in the United States only) have combined a domestic family limited partnership (FLP) with an offshore asset protection trust.

The combination of a domestic FLP and an offshore asset protection trust gives you more than one way to access assets. The interest from the limited partnership is transferred to the offshore trust while the trust retains legal ownership of the assets. A U.S. resident could control the assets as the general partner of the domestic **partnership**. As a general partner, you have access to the assets through either distributions of partnership capital, compensation for serving as the general partner, or loans from the partnership. You can control and recover the assets without having to dismantle your asset protection structure.

e. PLANNING THE DISTRIBUTION OF YOUR ESTATE

A major concern for many people is how their estate will be distributed after their death. But estate planning involves much more than just distribution under the terms of a will, trust, or inheritance law. Other things to consider include minimizing probate court costs and estate taxes, deciding who will care for your children, appointing people to handle your medical and financial affairs if necessary, and taking care of other financial, business, and personal responsibilities. While this can be a difficult subject to deal with, proper estate planning can save you and your family or business associates a great deal of money, pain, and confusion.

Your estate includes all assets and liabilities, and all property. Property is either "real" or "personal." Real property includes things such as real estate, while personal property includes physical assets such as automobiles, equipment, and household items. Personal property also includes financial property, such as securities, notes or loans receivable, bank accounts, cash, and insurance policies.

Planning your estate includes effective methods of holding property during your lifetime and passing your estate on to your heirs however and whenever you choose. Good planning should minimize taxes, reporting requirements, and legal or government intervention. Offshore structures and offshore financial centers can greatly simplify estate planning, and can substantially reduce — sometimes even eliminate — expenses, taxes, and legal hurdles.

f. OFFSHORE ADVANTAGES FOR ESTATE PLANNING

When you plan your estate, different types of offshore structures can give you certain advantages not available through domestic structures alone.

1. Foreign trusts

Both an offshore trust and a revocable domestic trust can help you avoid probate. However, in many instances, the offshore trust costs less. Offshore trusts can provide substantial asset protection benefits that domestic trusts can't. These benefits, such as the more favorable laws of the offshore jurisdiction being applicable over those of the domestic jurisdiction, produce stronger deterrents against possible creditors or spousal property claims on a divorce, and forced heirship rules under domestic law, and provide better security for the assets. Careful planning must take place to ensure domestic tax considerations are understood, and this can be influenced by whether you are a U.S. or Canadian resident/citizen and any special circumstances. If you establish a foreign trust for asset protection purposes, you do not also need to establish a separate domestic trust to avoid probate.

2. Offshore corporate structures

When you hold assets under an appropriately structured foreign corporate structure such as an IBC (which, unlike a person, never dies), you can indicate the succession of assets as easily as specifying the succession of signing authority on the corporate bank accounts and/or trading accounts.

Offshore trust and corporate structures are especially advantageous in both Canada and the United States, where laws allow for possible taxation from 32% to 55% on the transfer of an estate to heirs. These taxes are applied on property that you acquired with after-tax dollars, so the estate tax results in double taxation for your heirs. By incorporating offshore structures into your estate planning, you can substantially reduce the estate taxes payable and avoid double taxation.

8
COSTS OF STRUCTURING OFFSHORE

a. OVERALL COSTS

The costs of establishing and maintaining your offshore structures or vehicles vary depending on the quality of the structure, the jurisdictions' requirements, the amount of customization you need, and your use of professional help. Some offshore service providers will reduce their fees for structuring your trust, bank account, or company if you are also interested in holding your investment portfolio with them. The basic costs of **structuring offshore** generally fall into four categories:

(a) Identifying and customizing your agenda
(b) Setting up your offshore structure
(c) Maintaining your structure
(d) Administering your structure and obtaining ongoing professional advice

1. Identification and customization of your agenda

Identifying and customizing your agenda usually accounts for 20% to 30% of your costs. This is an important stage for several reasons. You should ensure you maximize your off-shore structure's benefits, and that the structure meets your personal or corporate needs. If your structure is not set up correctly, domestic tax authorities will also hold you individually or corporately responsible for everything, including taxes.

2. Setup

Establishing the structures themselves is frequently only one component of the cost in a properly structured offshore plan. Setting up offshore structures accounts for approximately 50% to 60% of the cost.

Almost anyone with a photocopy machine and word processor can create a company document or edit a foreign trust document. However, only a lawyer, licensed trust company, or bank can officially form corporations and trusts. It is important to make sure that the structure complies with the laws of the foreign jurisdiction. Your structure's legitimacy also depends on appropriate registration and maintenance. When these things are done properly, the integrity of your structures is secure and you can enjoy peace of mind. Usually, however, it means that you have to hire professionals, which can create significant costs depending on the complexity of the structure you require.

3. Maintenance

A structure that is properly set up should not have high maintenance costs; an average annual cost of between $200 and $5,000 a year is considered acceptable, depending on the structure and assets involved (e.g., is there an active trustee? Is a nominee director required?). If your offshore service provider wants a large annual percentage of your asset base or large ongoing fees, you should discuss it with him or her. Sometimes high annual fees are necessary and acceptable if your service provider's involvement is ongoing or if your investment is in a treaty jurisdiction that requires frequent attention to comply with the criteria of a certain treaty or concession.

4. Administration and ongoing professional advice

Administrative costs usually amount to 10% to 15% of the setup cost of a structure. Different jurisdictions have different administrative requirements. It's a good idea to ensure that your offshore service provider can offer you local expertise as well as a local presence. In the future, you may need his or her advice and consultation. As laws change and your investment agenda changes and expands, your offshore structures will have to serve different needs. Choose an offshore service provider that has an all-encompassing range of services rather than one that is either not able to answer your questions on an ongoing basis or that charges excessive hourly fees for consultation.

b. THE COST OF DOING IT RIGHT

Cheaper does not necessarily mean better. When you establish an offshore structure or engage an offshore service provider, the bitterness (and consequences) of poor quality will last far longer then the sweetness of low costs. Make sure you are comfortable with your offshore service provider in terms of his or her ability to provide high-quality service at a reasonable price. If the costs seem excessive, ask why. Your service provider may be considering his or her own interests first. At the same time, special circumstances may justify high costs.

Reasonable structure costs for most offshore agendas (in both treaty and nontreaty jurisdictions) should fall into the following ranges. Individual investors will most likely fall into the lowest range while complicated international corporate structures will likely fall into the higher ranges.

All amounts are in U.S. dollars.

(a) Company formation costs (variable according to jurisdiction and agenda): $750 to $20,000+.

(b) Trust establishment costs (depending on jurisdiction and type of trust): $2,500 to $30,000+.

(c) Bank account setup (depending on level of service and type of account): $100 to $600.

(d) Customization costs: $500 to $10,000 for an individual and $2,000 to $50,000 for a corporation.

Complex structures are more costly and time-consuming to construct than simple ones. If you have complicated tax, asset protection, estate planning, investment, or legal requirements, your structures may cost as much as 20% more than the above figures indicate. With large portfolios, a complicated structure may offer proportionately greater advantages than a simple, inexpensive one and can outweigh the high costs.

It is vital to ensure that your offshore structure meets your immediate and long-term needs. Make sure that you assign control appropriately, mitigate any risks, and, perhaps most important, that the structure conforms to both domestic and foreign laws. The peace of mind these assurances bring may come at the price of having a qualified professional customize your structure according to your needs. However, the costs of hiring a professional advisor will outweigh the cost of an improper structure, which can involve potential fines, problems with a tax authority, or losing control of your assets. Take the time and expense to deal with a qualified, reputable offshore professional who has an appropriate accounting, legal, and banking background.

c. IS IT WORTH THE COST?

Deciding how much to spend setting up your offshore structure depends on your or your company's agenda.

Generally, most individuals and corporations find that the breakeven point — when the savings pay for the costs — is much lower then they expect.

As a rough indicator, if your tax savings in the first year are greater than the offshore setup cost, your offshore services are worth the expense. In future years, your offshore structure costs will be very low and your financial savings will continue to grow. Even if you reach only the breakeven point, structuring offshore is well worth it when you consider the long-term payback — whether in the form of tax advantages, asset protection, estate planning, business purposes, or improved investment return.

If you are structuring offshore for investment growth and investments free from capital gains tax, $100,000 is typically the minimum portfolio you will need to break even on the offshore structure costs. Portfolios over $200,000 will see substantial advantages immediately and compounded benefits over time.

If instead you are structuring offshore vehicles for asset protection or estate planning, then the breakeven point is more ambiguous. An offshore service provider can help you better understand the extent of the asset protection or estate planning advantages offshore can offer you, and then you can compare the benefits and the costs.

9

HOW INDIVIDUALS
CAN TAKE ADVANTAGE OF
OFFSHORE FINANCIAL CENTERS

Chapter 1 outlined the broad benefits of structuring your affairs offshore. This chapter offers some examples of how specific individuals can use these benefits. Again, be sure to plan your investment strategy with a professional advisor.

a. INDIVIDUALS WITH INHERITED WEALTH

Individuals who inherit wealth can use offshore structures to reduce their inheritance taxes by converting the inheritance into money in low- or no-tax jurisdictions instead of in high-tax jurisdictions. They can also restructure the income their inherited portfolio generates so as to protect their assets and so that the income compounds tax free. If you structure your pre-inheritance wealth, it will simplify the succession process.

b. ENTREPRENEURS

Entrepreneurs who start off with an offshore structure can receive strategic benefits. Offshore offers entrepreneurs enhanced investment returns, access to global markets, better after-tax profits, and improved risk mitigation. An offshore vehicle can own corporate assets without exposing the entrepreneur's personal assets — this also reduces business risk. As well, if an entrepreneur structures his or her new venture offshore, it will survive the life of the original entrepreneur and simplify the succession process.

c. EXECUTIVES

Executives can use offshore for various aspects of their corporate agendas. Offshore can also help them restructure their compensation and stock programs so as to take advantage of reduced tax, asset protection, and access to global markets.

d. ENTERTAINERS AND AUTHORS

If entertainers and authors properly structure an offshore corporation to receive their contracts, they can reduce the tax they would otherwise owe. The offshore corporation earns income, and the entertainer or author is compensated for services rendered to that company.

e. ATHLETES

Athletes can use offshore benefits in the same way entertainers and authors can. By properly arranging personal compensation contracts with an offshore corporation, athletes can reduce the amount of tax they would otherwise owe onshore. Since the offshore corporation earns the income, the athlete is compensated for services rendered to that company.

f. OWNERS OF INTELLECTUAL PROPERTY

By assigning intellectual property rights and innovation rights to an offshore corporation, inventors, engineers, and designers can ensure revenue and royalties are received through an offshore corporation (as the owner of such rights) rather than have these revenues come to them personally. This reduces their personal tax obligation and protects their assets. Also, the intellectual property can remain offshore indefinitely, surviving the life of the original inventor. The inventor can easily specify the succession of what would otherwise have been his or her intellectual property rights.

The offshore company can arrange contracts to supply the invention or innovation outside the home country of the intellectual property owner. The offshore company earns the income the contracts generate, and this income can accumulate and compound, free from taxation, in the offshore center.

g. MEDICAL PRACTITIONERS AND OTHER PROFESSIONALS

Contracts for professional services often use offshore vehicles. Medical practitioners and other professionals use this technique to effectively restructure how their income is generated and realized, which reduces the personal tax they owe. Offshore vehicles also protect personal assets from professional business risks and malpractice claims.

h. INTERNATIONAL INVESTORS

Offshore companies can act as holding areas for investments made in a number of different markets and countries. You can collect all your investments together and have one offshore company hold legal ownership of them all. Personal holding companies can provide privacy and may save you the professional fees and other costs associated with setting up and maintaining a number of different offshore structures. Offshore entities allow your portfolio access to a variety of quality investment options that improve diversification and reduce risk. Investors regularly use offshore companies in personal portfolios for inheritance planning and to reduce the costs and time delays of probate.

10

HOW CORPORATIONS
CAN TAKE ADVANTAGE OF
OFFSHORE FINANCIAL CENTERS

Most modern corporations — home-based businesses, medium-sized companies pursuing international expansion, multinational companies, conglomerates, import-export companies, or financial institutions — are market driven. This means that their prices and costs are determined by a free market. They must compete with similar corporations to attract clients and consumers. Many have been able to establish and maintain their competitive edge by structuring some aspects of their operations through offshore centers. Some ways of doing this are through —

- Intellectual property and royalties reassignment
- Lease backs and leasing
- Options, futures, equity, and commodity trading
- Tax credit mixing
- Factoring and invoice discounting
- Purchasing and financing from offshore
- Importing and exporting
- Senior management compensation packages
- Equity ownership
- Patent and trademark registration
- Insurance and reinsurance
- Confidential transactions

- Trade and trade finance
- International investment
- Foreign transactions

Holding companies, foreign direct-investment companies, mixing companies, royalty companies, and treasury management companies are only a few examples of the types of companies that corporate users establish in offshore centers. Treasury management operations typically include cash management, capital raising exercises, the provision of finance to subsidiaries, and risk management. Corporate treasurers often divide their cash resources among their subsidiaries. This process is regularly undertaken from an offshore center.

Many corporate users favor establishing a physical presence in offshore centers. They might locate their regional headquarters, manufacturing and assembly plants, or marketing, trading, and administration centers offshore. They frequently use offshore centers for:

- Re-export and trans-shipping
- Transportation and distribution
- Factoring
- Invoice purchasing

Offshore facilities can offer corporations many interesting options. Some of the types of activities your offshore company can engage in are discussed in more detail below.

a. PROFESSIONAL MANAGEMENT

Many corporations establish a professional management company offshore to provide services and staff worldwide. You might give your offshore company exclusive rights to your professional services. The offshore company would receive payments for contracting out your services and pay you for the services you actually provide to the company. The company could then invest its profits in a low- or no-tax environment, instead of the high-tax environment of your home country.

b. INVESTMENT HOLDING

Many assets — stocks, bonds, mutual funds, and other movable and immovable investment products — can be consolidated in an offshore investment holding company while the income is realized offshore. This provides for tax-free compounded growth in the investments.

c. INTELLECTUAL PROPERTY

Royalties and licensing fees for intellectual property (e.g., computer software, technical knowledge, patents, trade-marks, trade secrets, and copyrights) can be owned by or assigned to an offshore company. When the offshore com-pany acquires the rights, it can then enter into license or franchise agreements with other companies interested in exploiting those rights around the world. You can let the income arising from this arrangement accumulate offshore in a tax-free environment. By the careful selection of a juris-diction and the use of double-taxation treaties, you can also reduce withholding taxes on royalty payments.

d. SALES OR INVOICING

Offshore entities may sell goods or services for parties throughout the world. Profits will accumulate in a tax-free environment.

e. LEASING

An offshore leasing company can own equipment and lease it to an onshore entity. This allows you (the onshore enti-ty) to take advantage of tax deductions on lease payments.

f. ADVERTISING

An offshore company that is an advertising agency can realize tax-free agency commissions offshore. The onshore company that commissions the advertisements can deduct the costs of the offshore advertising agency's fees.

g. MANAGEMENT SERVICES

Offshore entities can assume a variety of management and administration roles for onshore entities. The expenses are tax-deductible onshore.

h. CONSULTING

Consultants in almost any field of expertise may use an offshore company to arrange contracts with clients. By using the offshore company, the consultant can work as a representative of that company. Clients pay their fees to the offshore company rather than directly to the consultant.

i. PROPERTY

An offshore company can own real estate. This can reduce capital taxes and inheritance taxes, and simplify a variety of other complex issues onshore.

j. INTERNATIONAL TRADING AND PURCHASING

You can enjoy significant tax-saving opportunities by using an offshore company as a mediator in an international trading transaction. If an offshore company purchased products from one country and sold them to another country, the profits arising from the transaction may accumulate in the offshore company, free from taxation in the offshore center.

k. PUBLIC COMPANY OWNERSHIP

An offshore company can own share interests in onshore public companies.

l. FINANCE

Using offshore for finance is extremely attractive. Offshore finance companies can fulfill intra-company and inter-company financial management functions, such as lending money or financing projects. Interest payments from onshore companies to these offshore companies may be subject to withholding taxes, but often these taxes are different than the corporation taxes usually levied. In these cases, the interest paid would be a tax-deductible charge.

11

SELECTING AN OFFSHORE LOCATION

There are many factors to consider when choosing an offshore location. This chapter covers the major issues affecting the use of offshore financial centers, including political, economic, and legal factors, as well as the internal characteristics of various locations. It is important to research offshore locations thoroughly, with the help of a financial advisor, and to choose the jurisdiction that best meets your financial and business objectives.

a. POLITICAL STABILITY

Even though your funds or assets may never be physically in the offshore jurisdiction, the political stability of your offshore location is a vital concern. As offshore locations become increasingly competitive and generate more and more revenue, offshore jurisdictions will continue to attract investors because their advantages far outweigh any risks associated with structuring offshore. Although such risks are fewer today than they were in the past, sometimes external influences may disrupt the political stability of an offshore location. By appropriately structuring your offshore entities, you can make the risks of political instability significantly less severe. You can design your offshore corporations and trusts to be mobile and stable, or even so that political disruptions cannot affect them. The Bahamas and the Cook Islands, for example, have purposely structured their trust laws to create stability.

b. ECONOMIC STABILITY

Many offshore jurisdictions currently have some form of domestic exchange controls. This means they will allow exemptions from domestic economic laws and there may be different laws for foreign corporations, trusts, investors, and individuals.

Many jurisdictions have made a concerted effort to promote provisions that allow you to hold assets in any foreign currency. This way, your holdings aren't subject to the offshore jurisdiction's economic fluctuations. Many European-based banks are receptive to multicurrency accounts.

c. PROTECTORATES

A number of offshore jurisdictions are protectorates of other countries and have adopted laws very similar to those of their protector. The protector/protectorate relationship is important to offshore planners because it often explains the political and legal structure of the country and can be a good indication of the country's stability and security. A protectorate often has some clearly defined and limited political ties to the protector country.

Jersey, Guernsey, Bermuda, the Bahamas, and formerly Hong Kong are all protectorates of Britain. The United States, France, Holland, Spain, and several other countries also have protectorates.

d. CURRENCY

Offshore centers frequently use the domestic currency of the offshore jurisdiction. Many offshore domestic currencies are under exchange controls and their exchange rates are often linked to the U.S. dollar, British pound sterling, or similarly popular currency. However, for the purpose of offshore financial affairs and international businesses, most if not all banks, IBCs, and trusts operate free from exchange controls and in the currency of their choice. The U.S. dollar is probably the most popular currency for business and investments, but most institutions deal in up to 35 other major currencies, including:

Australian dollar	Hong Kong dollar
Austrian schilling	Indian rupee
Belgian franc	Irish punt
Bermudan dollar	Italian lira
Brazilian real	Japanese yen
British pound	Jordanian dinar
Canadian dollar	New Zealand dollar
Danish krone	Norwegian krone
Deutsch mark	Portuguese escudo
Dutch guilder	Saudi Arabian riyal
Euro dollar	Singapore dollar
Finnish markka	Spanish peseta
French franc	Swedish krona
Greek drachma	Swiss franc

e. CHOOSING A JURISDICTION

A number of factors will determine your choice of an offshore jurisdiction. The following discussion outlines some characteristics to consider.

1. Location

Where you establish your offshore structure is seldom where you conduct your day-to-day personal or corporate business. To simplify your operations, however, you should be near the region where your activities are located. This means that you should have reasonable access to your offshore jurisdiction from North America, and more importantly, if you do business internationally, from the place outside North America where the primary business occurs. Characteristics of reasonable access usually include scheduled airline flights, small or no time zone differences, and a good communications network (discussed in sections **e.9.** and **e.10.**). If goods will be shipped to or from your offshore location, you should ensure that appropriate shipping routes are available.

2. Language

If your primary language is English, it's important that the people you deal with in your chosen jurisdiction are fluent in English. Most offshore centers can provide multilingual services. If your offshore service provider can communicate fluently in your primary language, he or she will be able to understand your instructions and requirements fully and perform them properly with a minimal risk of mistakes.

3. Business infrastructure

It is essential that your chosen jurisdiction have a well-developed business infrastructure. To assess its business infrastructure, ask yourself questions like these:

- Are there proper banking facilities?
- Are there adequate professional personnel?
- Is there a skilled and/or unskilled labor force?
- Although you do not have to visit your offshore location, is there a 24-hour, year-round, accessible airport?

4. Exchange controls

If you want to bring your funds back to the currency of the country you live in, the offshore jurisdiction you choose should not impose exchange controls on foreign companies and trusts. Preferably, it should also be unlikely that your offshore jurisdiction will impose such controls in the future.

5. Legal system

A legal system based on, or that emulates, English common law is the preferred legal system and will provide the best security for your offshore structure. Britain, the United States, and Canada have legal systems based on common law. When the legal system of your offshore jurisdiction is similar to English common law, lawyers, accountants, and other onshore professionals will understand and accept offshore structures more easily and advise you better than if the offshore legal system is unfamiliar.

6. Banking

The jurisdiction you choose should offer a comprehensive range of banking services and access to international banking facilities. While most offshore companies can bank anywhere in the world, many prefer to open corporate accounts in the jurisdiction where the company was incorporated.

7. Treaty network

Sometimes you will benefit from establishing your offshore structure in a jurisdiction that has a range of treaties with other jurisdictions. This strategically positions your personal or corporate portfolio to benefit from future treaty agreements. Furthermore, if you want to take advantage of any double-taxation treaty, you must establish your offshore structures in a treaty jurisdiction. This is essential for the minimization of withholding taxes, capital taxes, income taxes, and taxes on dividends and royalties. In many instances, particularly tax related ones, treaty jurisdictions are also considered more reputable than nontreaty jurisdictions.

If you want privacy and confidentiality more than you want mobility, you should choose a jurisdiction such as the Bahamas which refuses to sign treaties with other jurisdictions (except for treaties on criminal-related activities such as drug trafficking).

Assess the taxation implications of the business you intend to conduct offshore, and decide whether or not you need to use a treaty jurisdiction. Most general agendas don't need treaty jurisdictions, but sometimes treaties are desirable and offer many advantages.

8. Legislation

More than 52 jurisdictions have legislation that encourages the formation of offshore companies and trusts in their jurisdiction. Some jurisdictions have introduced new, modern corporate legislation specifically designed for international business. Others have amended existing domestic legislation to cater to offshore requirements. The most essential criteria are that the legislation be flexible and offer:

(a) low capital requirements,

(b) minimal or optional statutory filing obligations,

(c) the ability to hold directors' and/or shareholders' meetings anywhere in the world,

(d) the ability to appoint professional directors, officers, and nominee shareholders,

(e) provisions allowing bearer shares to be issued,

(f) the absence of, or the optional requirement for, an audit of accounting records, and

(g) confidentiality and complete privacy in offshore business dealings.

TABLE 6: JURISDICTIONS FOR SPECIAL PURPOSES

CAPTIVE INSURANCE
Anguilla
Antigua
Aruba
Barbados
Bermuda
British Virgin Islands
Cayman Islands
Gibraltar
Guernsey
Ireland (Dublin)
Isle of Man
Jersey
Malta
Panama
Turks and Caicos Islands

MUTUAL FUNDS
Aruba
Bahamas
Barbados
Bermuda
British Virgin Islands
Cayman Islands
Ireland (Dublin)
Isle of Man
Guernsey
Jersey
Luxembourg
U.S. Virgin Islands

LIMITED LIFE COMPANIES
Anguilla
Antigua
Bahamas
Barbados
British Virgin Islands
Cayman Islands
Cook Islands
Isle of Man
Jersey
Mauritius
Samoa
St. Kitts–Nevis
St. Vincent
Turks and Caicos Islands
U.S. Virgin Islands

INVESTMENT OBJECTIVES
Guernsey
Ireland (Dublin)
Jersey
Liechtenstein
Luxembourg
Malta

Most jurisdictions create basic offshore legislation that is advantageous for company, banking, and trust agendas. Many jurisdictions also create legislation for more specific agendas. This "niche" legislation can be particularly suitable for individuals or corporations that are interested in **captive insurance,** limited life companies, mutual funds, or investment objectives. Table 6 lists some jurisdictions that offer niche legislation.

9. Communications
Your offshore jurisdiction must have good communications facilities so that you can conduct business efficiently and confidently. These facilities should include reliable air travel, mail services, and telecommunications systems.

10. Time zones
You will find it convenient if the offshore jurisdiction you choose has a time zone similar to that of your home country. Similar working hours will facilitate telephone communication between people both onshore and offshore during the business day. As competition to attract investors increases, some offshore locations have started providing around-the-clock services.

12

FREQUENTLY ASKED QUESTIONS

This chapter addresses some common concerns of many people new to offshore. For more specific information, you should discuss your situation with a financial advisor.

Who should I appoint as a trustee, beneficiary, and nominee director? How should I choose?
Most reputable offshore service providers will be able to help you choose a suitable trustee, beneficiary, and/or nominee director. Your choice will depend on the specific situation and agenda for which you are creating the structure. Often, trust firms, banks, investment firms, and professional service providers can offer trustee and nominee director services themselves. The fees for these services vary depending on the level of involvement you want your trustee or director to have, or the activities you want them to undertake.

Generally, a trustee or director should be chosen on the basis of your comfort with him or her, and his or her reputation, reliability, and ability to meet your needs. Take the time to assess which individual or corporation will best meet these expectations. Good choices will help affirm the legitimacy of your structure and ensure that your structure adequately meets your ongoing needs.

How do I buy foreign company shares from offshore?
You can buy shares in some major foreign companies on Canadian exchanges, and more major foreign companies offer shares on the U.S. exchanges. But there are thousands of companies to choose from on foreign stock exchanges. To be truly internationally diversified, you'll have to buy several stocks. Making a well-informed choice isn't easy, and sometimes it can be difficult to access information on companies quickly enough. As well, political, economic, and currency risks can lead to substantial changes in the value of your investment.

When you choose an offshore jurisdiction, consider the number and quality of investment firms available. You will want convenient communication with your offshore financial service provider and investment advisor, and access to foreign markets from your offshore jurisdiction.

How do I get real diversification — and manage my risk?
Studies have shown that adding some diversified foreign content may help reduce risk as well as improve performance over time. You can use this to your advantage by choosing offshore and domestic investments for your portfolio.

One way you can diversify is by investing in a variety of foreign stocks within a professionally managed mutual fund. A mutual fund investment allows you to diversify your portfolio with a much smaller investment.

Isn't there a lot of risk investing globally?
Yes. International investing also involves different risks than does domestic investing. Some of these risks include exchange rate fluctuations, different regulatory climates, and the increased potential for political instability. On the other hand, some of the world's oldest and most stable

financial markets exist in other countries. And many of the world's largest, soundest, and fastest-growing companies are found overseas.

Diversification can help you manage your risk exposure. Different investments move up and down at different times. Investing in several global industries and geographic areas can help moderate an individual market's effect on your overall portfolio. Most international and global mutual funds are broadly diversified and so using mutual funds can give you a head start on your diversification strategy.

How much of my portfolio should be in global investments?
The ratio between global and domestic investments varies with the needs and plans of each person — and his or her attitude toward risk. Among international mutual funds, it's generally true that the wider the scope of possible investments, the lower the risk. A truly global fund has lower risk because it's more widely diversified than one that looks at just one country or region.

Can I use the Internet to invest offshore?
The Internet is becoming an excellent tool for international and offshore investors. If the online investment site is properly structured (with SSL encryption technology and digital server certificates, which are both quickly becoming common features), it should be both safe and efficient. More and more brokerage firms and exchanges are moving to Internet-based clearing services and online financial services. The Internet lets you manage your offshore portfolio with the click of a button, from the comfort of your home. This has substantially reduced physical barriers to international investing and allows investors to stay informed and make profitable investment decisions. Offshore investors can also use the Internet to develop their knowledge and understanding of foreign jurisdictions, investment products, and the investing process.

The offshore structures discussed in this book lend themselves very well to online investment accounts, but careful review of onshore tax considerations is required. Often, setting up an offshore online account is as simple as filling out an online form and answering a few questions. You will find many reputable online investing firms by searching the Internet, and more appear every day. There are even online investing firms that deal exclusively with offshore-based clients — of online firms, these ones usually provide the widest range of investment options and the greatest level of privacy.

Is there a limit to how many offshore centers I can use?
No specific laws require you to use a minimum or maximum number of offshore centers. However, different jurisdictions have different advantages. Depending on your agenda, you may find it useful to use two, three, four, or even five different jurisdictions in your offshore structure. Using two or three jurisdictions in an average offshore structure is very common — one for the corporations, one for the trust, and one for the bank account. This three-level arrangement allows your offshore structure to take advantage of the best laws of each country and provides the maximum level of privacy.

Since the costs of using multiple jurisdictions are usually not excessive, many offshore structures adopt a multijurisdictional approach. Individuals or corporations with large portfolios or more than one reason for going offshore may need several separate structures, each in a different jurisdiction. For example, you might establish a company and trust structure in a private non-treaty area to handle estate planning and asset protection for your personal assets, and another company and trust structure for business needs in a jurisdiction that has favorable treaties with a jurisdiction you do business with.

If I decide I don't want or need an offshore structure any more, how can I dissolve it?

Most offshore structures can be revoked or dissolved very easily. Either the corporate documents or the offshore jurisdiction's corporate or trust laws should specify the dissolution procedure. Dissolving a structure usually costs no more than a small filing fee or a few hours of a lawyer's time. Even in circumstances where dissolving a structure is costly, you can simply remove all the assets from the structure, so it has zero value. You can then leave the empty structure to be stricken from the jurisdiction's register — a cost-effective way to eliminate it.

To ensure that your structure meets your needs now and in the future, and that you can change or eliminate the structure if it ever ceases to meet those needs, review the corporate documents and laws of the jurisdiction in which you choose to set up your structure. They will usually clearly state the dissolution process and give you a good idea of any costs associated with it.

For how long can I enjoy offshore asset protection, estate planning, and tax advantages?

Although laws change, there is currently no limit on how long offshore assets can be held or on how long offshore structures can remain in place. A properly structured offshore matrix can allow you to hold investments, real estate, and other assets indefinitely. These structures let individuals and corporations grow their assets tax free, protect them, and pass them on to the next generation.

OFFSHORE LOCATIONS

Part II of this book reviews several offshore jurisdictions. While many other offshore locations exist, the ones covered here are the offshore locations most commonly used by North American investors. For information on jurisdictions not discussed in this book or for more information on any of these jurisdictions, contact an offshore service specialist.

Each location has been given an overall rating based on its company, trust, and banking features combined with our experience and professional opinion. The ratings have been assigned with a North American focus.

As well as being given an overall rating, each jurisdiction's company, trust, and banking benefits have been rated based on our experience and professional opinion.

The ratings are —

★	Offers some basic opportunities for limited agendas
★★	Offers some basic opportunities for specific agendas
★★★	Average, typical, reliable advantages for an offshore jurisdiction
★★★★	Excellent, well-designed, stable, and effective advantages for most agendas
★★★★★	Jurisdiction of choice for that specific area (i.e., companies, trusts, banking)

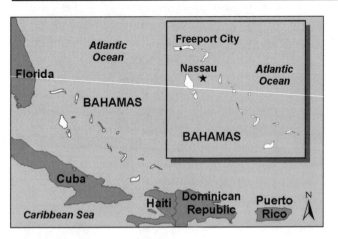

Overall rating: ★★★★
Companies: ★★★★
Trusts: ★★★★★
Banking: ★★★★

Type of jurisdiction: No tax.

Location: The Bahamas comprises a group of islands in the Atlantic Ocean situated 60 miles (96 kilometers) from the United States. The capital is Nassau, and most of the population lives on the islands of New Providence and Grand Bahama.

Population: Approximately 285,000.

Official language: English.

Currency: Bahamian dollars (BSD), which are pegged to the U.S. dollar at BSD 1 = USD 1. However, mainly U.S. dollars are used in international business and investments.

The Bahamas is used as an offshore location for the following reasons:
* It has an exemplary infrastructure.
* There is an established and globally integrated banking system.
* It has economic and political stability.
* There are flexible company laws.
* Corporate ownership can be in bearer share form.
* It has a reputable history of providing professional services.
* Companies are immediately available.
* It has a reputation as a solid financial center, with laws concerning taxes and asset protection.
* There are no double-taxation agreements with any other country.

Political and legal structure
The Bahamas has been independent since July 1973, but it has maintained its links with the British Commonwealth and has a common law system. The United Bahamian Party, Labour Party, Free National Movement Party, and Progressive Liberal Party compete for election to the 49 seats in the house of assembly and the 16 seats in the senate. The prime minister, who is also elected, governs with nine ministers appointed from the legislature.

Infrastructure and economy
Communication within the Bahamas is excellent. Regular flights to the Bahamas are posted by four major airlines, offering daily flights from a variety of locations. There are also charter flights. There are four commercial landing strips, with the airport on New Providence, Nassau International, receiving the majority of traffic. The proximity of the Bahamas to Miami accounts for the predominance of flights from Miami. There is also a world-class port in Freeport City with extensive shipping options.

Telecommunications are firmly in place, facilitating direct dial to the United States and Canada. There is also a new telex system and underground cables that run to West Palm Beach, Miami. Efficient courier and postal services are available.

Government income is generated through taxes on imports and customs duties. Although the Bahamas is a popular location for offshore services, tourism continues to account for the majority of its economic activity.

Exchange control
Exchange controls do not influence offshore services. Bahamian citizens are subject to exchange controls that discourage the holding of foreign currencies.

Companies
The 1866 Act regulates corporations used by Bahamian residents involved in local business dealings. The 1989 IBC Act specifies the tax exemptions for globally oriented companies that do not engage in local business dealings. Restrictions do not allow the ownership of property outside of that required for support of an office. A trust, insurance or reinsurance company, or bank cannot own property.

In addition, a Bahamian IBC must —
- have a registered address for its office;
- have an agent who is a registered solicitor, lawyer, management company, licensed trust company, or law firm;
- have two individuals or corporations as officers;
- issue currency of share capital in a way that is flexible and is available in nominal or **par value**; and
- have at least two individual or corporate shareholders.

IBCs are exempt from all Bahamian taxes for 20 years from the time of incorporation. License fees are due yearly and vary according to the share capital.

An IBC can be incorporated with any name that is not already taken but may not include words such as "Bank,"

"Building Society," "Chamber of Commerce," or any word that may indicate a connection with the British royal family or government. An IBC name can use the following suffixes to denote limited liability: "Limited," "Corporation," "Incorporated," "Société Anonyme," and "Sociedad Anonima."

Trusts

A trust is deemed to be a private matter in the Bahamas, which has strong modern trust laws, similar to that of England and other common-law jurisdictions. There are several ways to form a Bahamian trust. The trust document can vary in size, depending on its requirements and on the complexity of the provisions for transferring trust assets. The trust must be drawn up in such a way that there are options for extensive powers of discretion. The trust must furthermore be deemed resident or nonresident (for reasons of exchange control) and should clearly stipulate in pertinent documents of the trust the powers of the trustee.

Three forms of trusts are allowed in the Bahamas:
- Charity trusts for legally defined and legitimate charities that wish to access the no-perpetuity period of 80 years in the Bahamas
- Testamentary trusts, which become active only when a settlor dies and the estate receives assets
- Asset protection trusts, which may be irrevocable or revocable and nondiscretionary or discretionary

A series of legislative revisions have reinforced the desirability of establishing an offshore trust in the Bahamas. In 1989, the Trust Act declared that upon the explicit instructions from the settlor, Bahamian law will be the authority over the trust, to be accepted by the Bahamas courts. This act also provides the opportunity for the trust deed to alter the authority over the trust.

Banking

The Bahamas has a reputable and stable banking history that has encouraged a number of the world's major banks to establish their Caribbean head offices there. Along with an efficient infrastructure and prime geographical location, the Bahamas also has favorable banking laws.

Confidentiality is strictly enforced through the Bank and Trust Company Regulatory Act and there are penalties for the inappropriate dissemination of information. There are, however, exceptions. Deposits in excess of USD 100,000 have reporting requirements and foreign jurisdictional authorities are allowed to inquire into banking arrangements if they can provide solid evidence of criminal activity.

BAHRAIN

Overall rating: ★★
Companies: ★★
Trusts: ★
Banking: ★★

Type of jurisdiction: No tax.

Location: Bahrain consists of a group of islands in the Persian Gulf, between Saudi Arabia and Qatar. The largest island is called Bahrain and the capital is Manama.

Population: Bahrain has a fast-growing population, currently at approximately 700,000.

Official language: Arabic, although English is widely used.

Currency: Bahraini dinars (BHD), which are linked to U.S. dollars at BHD 1 = USD 1, but U.S. dollars are prevalent in international business and investment.

Bahrain has been an independent state since 1971 and was a British protectorate before that. Bahrain has been ruled by the same family since 1782, although there has been a British influence on the political system.

There are three major reasons to consider Bahrain for offshore services:

- It is a good location for an offshore bank.
- Holding companies find Bahraini law favorable.
- A resident of another jurisdiction is not taxed on employment within Bahrain.

Political and legal structure

The Al Khalifa family rules Bahrain through an appointed council of ministers and the Amir (an Al Khalifa family member who is the chief executive and head of state). Bahrain is largely influenced by English common law and to some extent Islamic law. Recently, Bahrain has been influenced by the Egyptian civil law model.

Infrastructure and economy

The Bahraini economy is driven primarily by oil. The abundance of oil and the need to export it has resulted in the development of a solid infrastructure. The Ministry of Commerce and Agriculture encourages the location of offshore banks and companies in Bahrain, and these activities are leading to strong economic growth.

Exchange control

There are no applicable exchange controls.

Companies

Offshore services have been available to non-Bahrainis since 1977. Companies offering such services are incorporated according to the Commercial Companies Law of 1975. As is usual with exempt companies, offshore companies may not engage in business dealings with Bahrainis.

Trusts

Bahraini law does not have favorable provisions for setting up offshore affairs.

Banking

The Bahrain Monetary Agency regulates banking arrangements.

BARBADOS

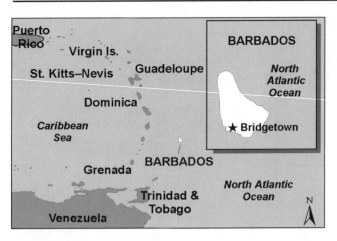

Overall rating: ★★★★
Companies: ★★★★
Trusts: ★★
Banking: ★★★★

Type of jurisdiction: Low tax.

Location: Barbados is an island of 166 square miles (430 square kilometers) in the eastern part of the Caribbean. Its capital is Bridgetown.

Population: Approximately 265,000.

Official Language: English.

Currency: Barbadian dollars (BBD), which have been pegged since 1975 at an exchange rate of BBD 2 = USD 1. Mainly U.S. dollars are used in international business and investment.

Barbados is a stable part of the British Commonwealth. It gained political independence in 1966 but continues its strong association with Britain. It is committed to favorable offshore policies. There are minimal business regulations and constraints in Barbados and it tries to maintain economic and political stability. Its association with the Commonwealth has influenced its political, judicial, and administrative systems, which reflect historical relations with Britain. Barbados also has a favorable tax treaty with Canada.

Political and legal structure

Barbados is committed to maintaining minimal business regulatory constraints and governmental interference in business. This has been reinforced by successive terms of the lower house and by the prime minister. A series of representatives, flowing from the Crown to the governor general to the members of the senate, consults with the prime minister and the opposition leader to make governmental decisions. The prime minister is elected through democratic election of the majority party, and an election is held every five years.

Infrastructure and economy

Barbados encourages private enterprise. It has enacted favorable corporate and investment laws and imposed minimal business constraints. In addition, there are no restrictions on owning assets or foreign-owned ventures. Barbados is a good location for profitable endeavors with limited government interference.

Barbados is an especially good location for access to the Canadian, U.S., European, and Caribbean markets. Through exemptions, Barbados has eliminated costs usually associated with jurisdictional trade. Barbados' infrastructure is equal to that of North America. There is a stable source of power and a network of telephones, roads, and ports.

Barbados provides an economy of operation with savings of 30% to 50% on U.S. or Canadian labor and manufacturing costs. Many products can be landed in the United States or Europe from Barbados at equal or lower total costs than Asian or Central American assembly.

Exchange control
The Central Bank of Barbados provides exemptions in the terms of exchange controls to offshore activities.

Companies
IBCs are regulated by the IBC Act of 1991 and the 1982 Companies Act. You must obtain a license, and your company will incur taxes on profits from global business. The tax rates range from 1% to 2.5% and up to 15% in treaty jurisdictions.

Corporate names must not be the same as an existing corporate name and may not include the words "Corporation," "Incorporated," or "Limited." Words such as "Cooperative," "Bank," and "Insurance" may be used only with the permission of the government.

Barbados has a treaty with Canada that makes it a very attractive jurisdiction in which to incorporate a company — the Canadian subsidiary will flow income into the Barbados parent at a maximum tax rate of 15%.

Trusts
Barbados has emulated the trust laws of Britain. The Trustee Act clearly defines the powers of trustees. If they reside within and manage the trust from Barbados, the trust is considered resident within Barbados. Trusts that are resident in another jurisdiction incur taxes only when income is transferred to Barbados by a nonresident settlor or beneficiary.

In 1995 the creation of the International Trust Act provided greater flexibility for implementing and managing trusts in Barbados. As well, the act clearly defines the law, establishes detailed trust characteristics, and offers the following useful guidelines and information for international trusts:

- Trusts for noncharitable purposes are defined and permitted.
- Unless stated otherwise, it is assumed that the trust is irrevocable.
- The trust terminates after 100 years (as opposed to the perpetuities constraint).
- Specific trusts, such as the purpose or charitable trust, which do not terminate after 100 years are provided for.
- The Barbados courts do not adhere to heirship laws imposed by other jurisdictions.
- All income generated from the trust can accumulate for 100 years.
- The dispositions of the property cannot be challenged after three years of disposition.
- The settlor can appoint a protector and define his or her role.
- Trustees are responsible for the provision of confidentiality.
- Beneficiaries of trust distributions and allocations who are nonresidents are tax exempt in Barbados.
- International trusts do not require registration.

Banking

Barbados has a well-developed banking infrastructure. Banking arrangements are diverse and cater to a wide variety of needs: commercial, offshore-related, and personal. All banks in Barbados are regulated and authorized for foreign currency transactions by the Central Bank of Barbados, which also governs monetary policies and exchange controls within the country. Nonresidents must receive permission from the central bank to borrow funds locally.

BERMUDA

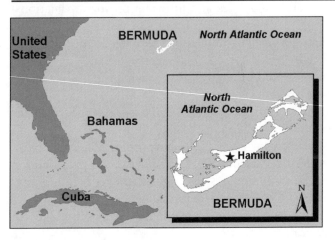

Overall rating: ★★★
Companies: ★★
Trusts: ★★
Banking: ★★★

Type of jurisdiction: No tax.

Location: Bermuda comprises a group of over 150 islands situated approximately 580 miles (930 kilometers) east of Cape North Carolina. There are seven principal islands, and the capital is Hamilton.

Population: Approximately 57,500.

Official language: English.

Currency: Bermuda dollars, which are tied to U.S. dollars at par. U.S. dollars are prevalent in international business and investment.

Bermuda has just one tax treaty, which is with the United States. This double-tax treaty provides for the exchange of information on tax frauds and evasions, thus limiting privacy and confidentiality of companies and trusts in Bermuda. However, Bermuda remains an excellent jurisdiction for insurance companies and reinsurance companies.

Political and legal structure

Bermuda was colonized by Britain in 1612 and remains the oldest self-governing colony within the British Commonwealth. The Bermudian Constitution Order provides for internal self-government, with England retaining responsibility for external affairs, defense, internal security, and the police. In keeping with most British colonies, Bermuda has adopted the English common law system.

Infrastructure and economy

Bermuda is exceptionally well developed, with good telecommunications, airport, and ports.

Tourism is the major industry, accounting for over 90% of the GDP.

Exchange control

Bermuda exercises its own independent controls under the regulations of the Exchange Control Act, 1972. Exchange control is administered by the exchange control department of the Bermuda Monetary Authority.

Companies

The Companies Act, 1981, amends and consolidates Bermuda company law. Bermuda companies fall into two main categories: companies incorporated by local businesspeople for trade and business in Bermuda and companies incorporated by non-Bermudians for the purpose of conducting business outside Bermuda from a head office located in Bermuda (known as exempt companies). An exempt company is restricted by the 1981 act to doing business only outside Bermuda.

Trusts
Trusts are set up in Bermuda under English common law, as amended in Bermuda. A modern trust is usually expressed by a written trust agreement or deed of settlement which details how the trust's capital and income are to be held, administered, and distributed. There are limited restrictions placed on the trust structure, and therefore most trust agreements are customized to accommodate the specific agenda.

The Trustee Act of 1975, which is similar to the English Trustee Act of 1925, sets out general provisions for the powers and duties of trustees. Trust agreements fall into two general classifications: fixed or discretionary. Fixed agreements detail precisely who will benefit under the trust arrangement and when, whereas discretionary-type trust arrangements grant discretionary rights to the trustees.

Most trusts established in Bermuda are discretionary. A common practice in Bermudian trusts is to enable the trustees to add further beneficiaries at a later date and to remove persons from the existing list of beneficiaries.

Banking
There are three commercial banks in Bermuda that offer full commercial banking services. The banks each have their own correspondents with major banks in financial centers around the world and are well equipped to handle business and financial transactions to all major currencies.

British Virgin Islands

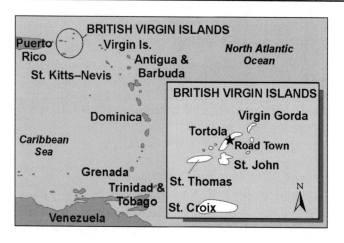

Overall rating: ★★★★
Companies: ★★★★★
Trusts: ★★★★
Banking: ★★★

Type of jurisdiction: No tax on foreign income.

Location: The territory of the British Virgin Islands (B.V.I.) consists of 40 islands near Puerto Rico, half of which are inhabited. The principal island is Tortola, and two-thirds of the population live in the capital, Road Town.

Population: Approximately 18,000.

Official language: English.

Currency: U.S. dollar.

The British Virgin Islands is an attractive offshore financial center for the following reasons:

- Zero-tax corporate status is available.
- Modern company formation law provides maximum flexibility.
- Historically, there has been political and economic stability.
- Banking, professional, and communications infrastructures are well developed.
- Bearer share ownership is permitted.

Political and legal structure

The jurisdiction of the British Virgin Islands is a British territory. The present constitution was established in 1967. There is an elected legislative council with a chief minister (who is selected from the 13 elected members), the attorney general (an ex-official member), and the speaker (who is elected to the legislative council from outside the assembly).

The legal system is based on common law and a significant proportion of British law has been adopted.

Infrastructure and economy

There is reliable daily air service to and from the island. Cruise ships call in weekly to the islands, and there is also a developed port. There are excellent telecommunications facilities and courier services.

The primary economy is tourism and the offshore financial services industry, especially company formation services.

Exchange control

There are no exchange controls in the British Virgin Islands.

Companies

The British Virgin Islands is by far the most popular jurisdiction in the world for company formation. There are three basic types of companies available: the CAP 285 resident company, the CAP 285 nonresident company, and the IBC. CAP 285 companies are governed by the amended Companies Act, 1885, which is now similar to the British Companies Act of 1948. Resident CAP 285 companies are established for domestic purposes only. A nonresident company is used when the proposed activity of the company needs to be licensed.

IBCs are governed by the IBC Act of 1984, one of the most modern corporate statutes in the world. An IBC can be incorporated with any name that is not already in existence, but may not include words such as "Insurance," "Assurance," "Building Society," "Bank," or "Trust." As well, the name cannot include words indicating a connection with the British royal family or government.

An IBC name can use one of the following suffixes to denote limited liability: "Limited," "Corporation," "Incorporation," "Société Anonyme," "Sociedad Anonima," or the relevant abbreviations. The articles of association govern the internal affairs of the company and may be changed by corporate resolution.

Trusts

The purpose of a trust in the British Virgin Islands ranges from asset protection and family estate planning to tax minimization. The most significant features of this modern trust law include —

- exemption from all forms of taxation,
- confidentiality, as there is no public register of trusts,
- maximum perpetuity period of 100 years,
- exclusion of forced heirship, and
- retention of wide management powers through the role of the protector.

Trusts can be drafted to suit the client's specific requirements. The types of trusts that can be formed include revocable or irrevocable trusts, short-form or long-form trust deeds, full discretionary or fixed-interest settlements, **accumulation** and maintenance settlements for minors and charities, and protective trusts to remove future creditor risks.

Trust law is based on the principles of equity as applied in Britain. The B.V.I. trust law can be found in the Trustee Ordinance Act of 1961.

Banking

Banking is regulated under the Banks and Trust Companies Act, 1990. This act controls banking business and places a licensing function on the minister of finance. The British Virgin Islands has limited banking facilities and is generally not considered a prime banking jurisdiction.

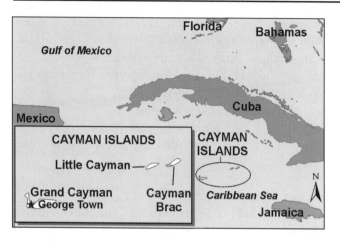

Overall rating: ★★★★★
Companies: ★★★★
Trusts: ★★★
Banking: ★★★★

Type of jurisdiction: No tax.

Location: The Cayman Islands consists of three islands in the Caribbean. The main island, Grand Cayman, is approximately 450 miles (720 kilometers) south of Florida, and the capital is George Town.

Population: The combined population of the three islands is approximately 27,000, the majority of which live on Grand Cayman.

Official language: English.

Currency: Cayman dollars, with one Cayman dollar having a fixed value of USD 1.20. However, U.S. dollars are prevalent in international business and investment.

The Cayman Islands are a solid no-tax haven with no direct taxation of residents or corporations. There are no capital gains, inheritance, or gift taxes, although there is stamp duty on real estate. The Cayman Islands' primary attractions as an offshore financial center are that —

- a modern and well-developed companies formation law provides maximum flexibility,
- bearer shares ownership is allowed,
- confidentiality laws are strong, and
- the banking and professional infrastructure are well developed.

Political and legal structure

The Cayman Islands is a British colony. The islands have a government that is appointed by the Queen and that is responsible for the civil service, defense, law and order, and external affairs. There is also a legislative assembly (composed of 12 elected members plus the financial secretary) and an executive council (consisting of three official members appointed by the governor and four members elected by the legislative assembly). This group formulates policy and advises the government.

The Cayman Island legal system is based on English common law and much of British law has been adopted.

Infrastructure and economy

There are excellent communication facilities in the Caymans. The islands are served by Cayman Airways, Northwest Airlines, and American Airlines. The islands are also a popular cruise ship stop.

The economy of the islands is strong, enjoying full employment. Most of the revenue comes from the financial services sector and tourism.

Exchange control

Offshore entities are exempt from exchange control conditions.

Companies

The Cayman Islands company law is based on the British Companies Act of 1948, which was amended in the 1960s, resulting in beneficial features distinct to the Cayman Islands.

There are three types of Cayman Islands companies: ordinary resident companies, ordinary nonresident companies, and exempt companies. These companies may be limited by shares or guarantee or may be unlimited. The most common type of company is the exempt company, which is used primarily by nonresidents for offshore purposes.

Companies can be incorporated using any name that is not considered undesirable by the registrar and are not permitted to include words such as "Royal," "Imperial," "Government," "Chartered," or any name that might imply a connection with government or the royal family. Other names such as "Bank," "Insurance," and "Trust" may not be used without registrar approval and the appropriate license.

Exempt companies may be suffixed with the words "Limited," "Incorporated," "Corporation," "Société Anonyme," or abbreviations to indicate limited liability.

All Cayman Islands companies are required to maintain a registered office address in the Cayman Islands. The minimum number of directors is one, and may be either an individual or corporation. The minimum number of shareholders is one.

An exempt company is required to hold at least one meeting a year in the Cayman Islands, although alternative directors may be used for this.

Trusts

The principal trust law is based on the U.K. Trustee Act of 1925 and the Variation of Trusts Act, 1958. While Cayman Islands trusts are similar to those of Britain, the major differences are that there is no rule against accumulations and that the rule against perpetuities has been modified to 150 years.

Banking

The Cayman Islands is renowned as a good place to set up banks. The banking law is specified in the Banks and Trust Companies Law of 1989. There are over 560 banks and trust companies licensed by the government to carry on business in the Cayman Islands — more than in any other financial center except for London and New York. Most major banks have representation in the Caymans.

The banking community and the government of the Cayman Islands have taken a strong stance against money laundering. It was with this in mind that the government signed the Mutual Legal Assistance Treaty in 1986 with Britain and the United States, which provides for the mutual exchange of information where there is evidence of criminal activity. However, tax matters are specifically excluded.

COOK ISLANDS

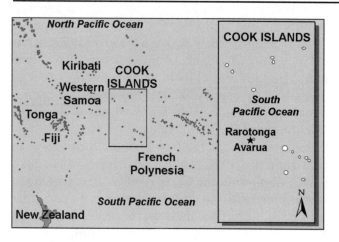

Overall rating: ★★★★
Companies: ★★★
Trusts: ★★★★
Banking: ★★★

Types of jurisdiction: No tax.

Location: The Cook Islands comprises 15 islands of the South Pacific. The main island is Rarotonga, where two-thirds of the population live. The capital is Avarua.

Population: Approximately 25,000.

Official language: English.

Currency: New Zealand dollars, but U.S. dollars are prevalent in international business and investment.

The territory known as Cook Islands was settled by Polynesian voyagers over 1,000 years ago and was administered by New Zealand until 1965. The country's development as an offshore finance center began in the early 1980s. It has attracted not only Asian client interest but also North American. Many features of its offshore legislation, such as those pertaining to asset protection and trusts, are technically innovative and maintain the Cook Islands as one of the world's leading offshore jurisdictions.

The Cook Islands was the first offshore jurisdiction to enact legislation under the International Trust Amendment Act of 1989. As a result, the Cook Islands currently has the most modern international trust legislation, with particular emphasis on the protection of assets, the protection of beneficiaries, and flexibility of control by the settlor.

Political and legal structure

In 1965, the New Zealand parliament passed the Cook Islands Constitution Act giving the Cook Islands self-governing rule and its own constitution. Today the Cook Islands has a parliamentary system based on that of Britain, with democratic elections held every five years.

There are two main political parties: the Democratic Party and the Cook Islands Party. Between them there are 25 seats in parliament. Both parties support the country's status as an offshore financial center.

The Cook Islands has a common law legal system, using the English common law of 1840 as its foundation. Some New Zealand legislation from the period during which the islands were administered by that country still applies.

Infrastructure and economy

The government has reaffirmed continuing support and encouragement for the development of Rarotonga as a financial center; this includes the development of Rarotonga's infrastructure.

The Cook Islands has growing international stature and is a member of the South Pacific Forum, the Asian Development Bank, and the Economic Commission for Asia and the Pacific.

Rarotonga has a well-developed telecommunications network. There are also good postal and courier services and an international airport with regular flights.

Exchange control

There is no exchange control in the Cook Islands.

Companies

The International Companies Act of 1981-1982 created the international company — the offshore corporate vehicle most commonly used in the Cook Islands. It is possible for a foreign company to register under the act in order to gain its benefits. When a company plans to be listed on a stock exchange, it may be registered as a registered listed company, but some of the general requirements that apply to international companies must be modified. Cook Islands international companies can be listed on the Hong Kong stock exchange.

The International Companies Act provides a legislative guarantee to international companies that they will not be subject to taxes. Also they are not subject to filing requirements except those of banks, insurance companies, and trust companies.

Trusts

The International Trusts Act of 1984 establishes a registration system for trusts and provides the trust with benefits and protection. Application for registration is made by a licensed trustee company. The application must specify that no resident of the Cook Islands is a beneficiary and must include the date of the trust deed, the name of the trustee, and the name of the trust. Under the act, information pertaining to an international trust, including the deed of trust and the identity of parties connected with the trust, is strictly confidential and subject to the secrecy provisions of the act.

The act creates a favorable environment in which the familiar British trust concept can be used for both tax planning and asset protection. The legislation eliminates many of the difficult aspects of common law relating to trusts. The perpetuity period may not exceed 100 years. Other common law rules, such as the rule against accumulations and double possibilities, do not apply.

Banking

Banking business in the Cook Islands may be carried on only by licensed banks that have received approval from the Cook Islands Monetary Board under the Banking Act of 1969 or the Offshore Banking Act of 1981.

The definition of banking contained in the Offshore Banking Act of 1981 and the amending Act of 1985 ensures that banks, merchant banks, and other financial institutions transacting offshore banking business must be licensed. Offshore banking business means banking business transacted by or for any person who —

(a) is not a resident in the Cook Islands, and

(b) does not engage in trade or business in the Cook Islands.

A licensed offshore bank, which may be either an international company or a domestic company, is exempt from all taxation and duties on its profits or gains derived from offshore banking business, as well as on the interest earned from this banking business. No taxation is imposed on interest paid to nonresident depositors nor on dividends or other earnings on securities beneficially owned by nonresidents (i.e., earnings of which nonresidents are the beneficiaries).

Specific confidentiality provisions are provided in the banking act and sanctions are imposed on government officials, officers, employees, and auditors disclosing information on the offshore banking business.

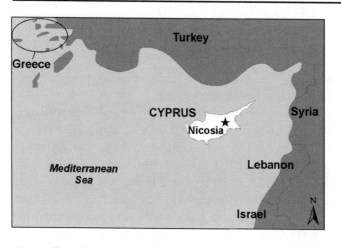

Overall rating: ★★★
Companies: ★★★
Trusts: ★
Banking: ★★★

Type of jurisdiction: Low tax.

Location: Cyprus is an island of approximately 3,900 square miles (10,100 square kilometers), situated in the Mediterranean Sea. Its capital is Nicosia.

Population: Approximately 725,000.

Official language: Greek and Turkish, but English is widely used, particularly for commerce.

Currency: Cyprus pounds (CYP), which are divided into 100 cents each.

Cyprus is an attractive offshore financial center as it has —
- attractive leasing laws for offshore entities,
- an extensive favorable double-taxation treaty network,
- a historically stable political and economical system, and
- an established banking, telecommunications, and professional infrastructure.

Cyprus has signed beneficial agreements for offshore parties with Britain, Bulgaria, Canada, Denmark, France, Germany, Greece, Hungary, Ireland, Italy, Kuwait, Norway, Russia, Sweden, and the United States. Agreements with Austria, Belgium, Egypt, Finland, India, and Mexico are in progress. Combining the existence of such treaties with the low rates of tax applicable to offshore companies operating from within Cyprus provide unique tax reduction opportunities.

Political and legal structure

Cyprus became an independent republic in 1960. It is a democracy with a president and a legislature referred to as the house of representatives. Its historical relationship with Britain has meant that its government, administration, and legal system have developed from English law. The Cyprus legal system is based on the same principles applicable in Britain, and all statutes regulating business matters and procedure are based on British law. Most laws are officially translated into English.

Infrastructure and economy

The Cyprus economy is based on a free enterprise system. The government's role is limited to planning, regulating, and providing basic utilities. During the last ten years, the economy of Cyprus has grown dramatically, and its currency has been relatively stable.

Agriculture is no longer the principal economic sector, although it remains the largest employer. Manufacturing now represents the largest proportion of the country's current GDP. Tourism also provides an important source of foreign income.

Cyprus has two airports, and there are frequent air connections to many international destinations. There are also major port facilities and well-developed roads. Cyprus has good telecommunications systems, and there are good postal and courier services.

Exchange control

The Cyprus Exchange Control Law prohibits residents of Cyprus from dealing in foreign currencies and imposes restrictions on importing or exporting currency. Foreigners require permission from the central bank to acquire shares in Cyprus companies.

Offshore companies and other entities acquire nonresident status on their formation or establishment, which means that they can move foreign currencies freely to and from Cyprus through their bank. There are regulations and controls to deter money laundering.

Companies

Cyprus corporate law is almost identical to Britain's Companies Act of 1948 and provides for the establishment of both private and public companies. To establish an offshore company in Cyprus, exchange control permission is required. As well, nonresidents require governmental permission to subscribe to shares in the company.

An offshore company can be incorporated using any name that is not considered undesirable by the registrar but may not include words such as "Bank" or "Insurance" without the appropriate license and also may not include words such as "National," "Imperial," "Commonwealth," "Cooperative," or "Worldwide." All company names must be suffixed with the word "Limited" to indicate limited liability.

Every company is required to maintain a registered office address in Cyprus. An offshore Cyprus company must have at least one person who is the director. Shares are generally issued with a par value of one Cyprus pound, although there is no legal minimum par value. Shares must be in registered form, and bearer shares are not permitted. There must be a minimum of two shareholders.

Trusts

Until 1992, Cyprus trust law was modeled on pre-1960 British law, which provided a tax-free status for offshore trusts. The International Trusts Law of 1992 introduced a special set of rules for international trusts. Other trusts are governed by the existing Trustees Law of 1955 and the rules of equity and trust law as applied in Britain.

Banking

Cyprus has an entrepreneurial, aggressive banking system. A number of the world's major banks are represented, and Cyprus has a good relationship with most world banks. It is a major banking center for Eastern Europe and is very positive toward venture loans.

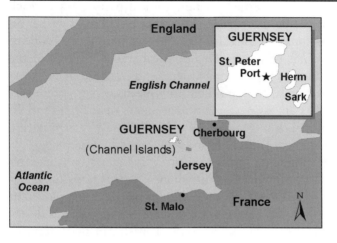

Overall rating: ★★★
Companies: ★★★
Trusts: ★★
Banking: ★★★★

Type of jurisdiction: No tax on foreign income.

Location: Guernsey, situated off the northwest coast of France near the Cherbourg Peninsula, in the Bay of St. Malo, is the second largest of the Channel Islands.

Population: Approximately 60,000.

Official language: English.

Currency: Pounds sterling, but U.S. dollars are prevalent in international business and investment.

Guernsey holds the territory under a bailiff, which also includes Alderney, Sark, and Herm.

Political and legal structure

Guernsey is governed on nonpolitical party lines — each member votes according to his or her electorate's wishes on a specific matter. Therefore, the government is not prone to wide swings of policy. This political stability is one of the major advantages to using Guernsey as a financial center.

Alderney, although reliant on Guernsey for certain services, has its own states and a small finance sector. In contrast, Sark is governed by chief pleas, a system dating back to feudal times. Herm is governed by Guernsey.

The simplicity of the Guernsey system is enhanced by the lack of capital gains, inheritance, capital transfer, value-added, or withholding taxes. One in six people employed in Guernsey works in the finance sector. Guernsey has designated territory status under the British Financial Services Act of 1986. This means that investor protection is as good as that in Britain.

Infrastructure and economy

To average European standards, Guernsey's infrastructure is well developed. The economy is focused primarily on financial services and the finance industry has a solid supporting infrastructure including banks, insurance companies, asset management services, stockbrokers, actuaries, accountants, lawyers, trust services, and company formation services.

Exchange control

Offshore entities use various currencies and are exempt from exchange control conditions.

Companies

Under the Income Tax Ordinance of 1989, Guernsey companies may be exempt from taxation. A director or secretary of the company must declare beneficial ownership to the Financial Services Commission and must state names and contact information of the beneficial owners of the company's shares. If those shares are held in trust, the declaration must state the names and addresses of the trustees, the settlor, and any other person who provided the trust property, as well as the name of the trust. The commission has the right to request the names of all people who have a beneficial interest in the company.

Trusts

Trusts have been constructed under Guernsey law for many years and, under the Trusts Law of 1989, they possess full statutory recognition. This law provides a flexible vehicle for many types of trusts, including protective trusts.

Banking

The use of banks for offshore purposes has been part of Guernsey's financial services since 1987, when the first banks were set up within the Ansbacher banking group. Today, Guernsey has 18 banks, all of which are run by qualified bankers. Guernsey does not allow banks to be run by nonbankers.

Guernsey-style administered banks (originally known as "managed" banks) have emerged as a way of expanding the island's banking industry and signaling to the international community that the island is open to new banking business.

HONG KONG

Overall rating: ★★★★
Companies: ★★★
Trusts: ★
Banking: ★★★★

Type of jurisdiction: Low tax.

Location: Hong Kong is southeast of the Chinese mainland and consists of a number of islands as well as part of the Chinese mainland.

Population: Approximately, 6.5 million. Hong Kong is the most densely populated area in the world.

Official language: English and Cantonese, with English being used mostly in the commercial and political context and Cantonese used widely in industry and domestic trade.

Currency: Hong Kong dollars (HKD), which are linked to U.S. dollars at the rate of HKD 7.80 = USD 1.00. U.S. dollars are prevalent in international business and investment.

Hong Kong is an attractive offshore financial center for a variety of reasons:

- Income earned outside Hong Kong is exempt from taxes.
- It has an excellent and reliable commercial, telecommunications, and banking infrastructure.
- It has well-developed company formation laws.
- There is no disclosure of beneficial owners or corporate details to the general public.

Because taxes are based on the source of income, Hong Kong is a low-tax jurisdiction rather than a no-tax jurisdiction. Therefore, Hong Kong is suitable for companies wishing to base themselves in Hong Kong but that have business and income outside Hong Kong.

Political and legal structure

A British colony for 99 years, Hong Kong is now part of the People's Republic of China. In 1984, an agreement was made between the British and Chinese governments that on July 1, 1997, Hong Kong would become a Special Administrative Region of China. The agreement guarantees the following for 50 years —

(a) A local government will continue and it will have full authority over executive, legislative, and judicial matters.
(b) The legal, social, and economic systems will remain in force.
(c) All forms of property, including inheritance and ownership by non–Hong Kong citizens, will be respected by the Chinese government.
(d) The Hong Kong dollar will continue to be the official currency.
(e) Hong Kong's financial system will remain independent, and China will not raise taxes in Hong Kong.
(f) Hong Kong will remain independent for customs purposes.

(g) Crown land leases may be granted for up to 50 years after 1997.

(h) The free port will remain.

While Hong Kong is able to negotiate economic relations with other countries and also control entry and exit, China is now responsible for its foreign affairs and defense.

Infrastructure and economy

Hong Kong's infrastructure is very well developed. Since Hong Kong is a small country, most business is concentrated in its central island region. The territory is Southeast Asia's center for trade, finance, and commerce.

Exchange control

There is no exchange control in Hong Kong.

Companies

The most common type of company in Hong Kong is one that is limited by shares, similar to the type of private company used in North America. Hong Kong companies may also be limited by a guarantee or may be unlimited. Hong Kong company law is based on the British Companies Ordinance of 1932 and has been amended to suit the country's needs.

A Hong Kong company can be incorporated with any name other than one that indicates a connection with the government or with a company that has already been formed. It must maintain a registered office address in Hong Kong. A log of directors, secretaries, shareholders, and corporate meetings must also be kept at the registered office.

A Hong Kong company must keep detailed accounting records. Every company must have an appointed auditor who must be a member of the Hong Kong Society of Accountants. There is a requirement to file the accounts with tax authorities.

Trusts

Hong Kong has adopted British trust law. The Hong Kong Trustee Ordinance is similar to the English Trustee Act of 1925. Legislation has also been formed to allow perpetuities and accumulations.

Banking

There is no central bank in Hong Kong. Banks are licensed by the banking commissioner under the Banking Ordinance, 1986. There is an extremely well-developed banking system in Hong Kong and the majority of the world's major banks are represented there.

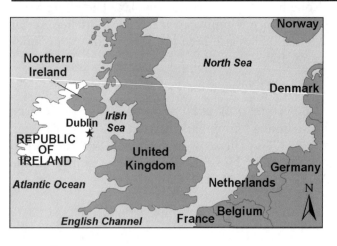

Overall rating: ★★★
Companies: ★★★
Trusts: ★
Banking: ★★★

Type of jurisdiction: Unique tax.

Location: The Republic of Ireland is situated to the west of the United Kingdom and separated from it by the Irish Sea. Roughly one-third of the population lives in the capital, Dublin.

Population: Approximately 3.5 million.

Official language: English; however, there are many areas, referred to as "An Gaeltacht," such as the Aran Islands, Connemara, Galway, and Cork, where Irish Gaelic is spoken.

Currency: Irish pounds or punts, which are linked to the European Monetary System. However, U.S. dollars are prevalent in international business and investment.

Although Ireland is not typically considered a low-tax jurisdiction, it is used in many offshore tax planning structures for a number of specific purposes. Ireland itself is not an offshore jurisdiction, but Dublin (the Shannon Free Trade Zone) is an offshore sector of the country. Ireland is a member of the European Union (E.U.). Recently, the use of nonresident Irish companies became popular after new U.K. resident companies could no longer be used as tax-reducing offshore companies. Ireland also has attractive investment fund legislation, although its E.U. membership limits confidentiality. Ireland has several favorable treaties for offshore purposes, especially for Canadians.

Political and legal structure

Until 1922, all of Ireland was part of the United Kingdom. Following a war of independence, Britain entered into a treaty with Ireland, and the island was partitioned into Northern Ireland and the Irish Free State. In 1949, the Irish Free State became a republic and left the British Commonwealth. Northern Ireland remains an integral part of the U.K.

The Republic of Ireland is a parliamentary democracy. The president is the head of state and is elected for a maximum of two terms of seven years. The parliament is known as the Oireachtas and consists of two houses: a lower house and the senate, or Seanad Eireann. The members of the senate are all elected by vocational panels such as farming, employer, union, educational, and commercial groups.

Infrastructure and economy

Airlines offer regular flights to all major airports. There are freight and ferry services available to Britain and France. Ireland has well-developed modern telecommunications facilities. Regular international courier services are operated by numerous companies.

Ireland's economy is small and dependent on trade. Agriculture once made up the majority of the GDP but is now dwarfed by industry, which accounts for 40% of the GDP, about 80% of exports, and employs 30% of the labor force.

Exchange control
Offshore entities are not subject to exchange controls in Ireland.

Companies
Irish company law is set out in the Companies Acts 1963-1990. As Ireland is not an offshore jurisdiction, the law has a certain degree of complexity. It has been influenced by corresponding U.K. law and more recently by the corresponding E.U. laws. It is still possible to have an Irish company that is nonresident for income tax purposes, but it should be noted that nonresident companies do not contain the special features that are found in the offshore companies of many of the true offshore jurisdictions.

Trusts
Ireland follows the British laws of trusts. Since 1992, trusts established in Ireland as offshore entities have been exempt from all Irish tax. The beneficiaries, however, must not be Irish residents or domiciled in Ireland, and the settlor must not be domiciled in Ireland when the trust is set up.

Banking
Ireland has a regulated banking system, with the Central Bank of Ireland as the controlling authority.

The establishment of the International Financial Services Centre in Dublin and the Shannon Free Trade Zone has made it possible to establish offshore banking subsidiaries in them which are subject to tax at a maximum of 10%, along with other advantages. The confidentiality of Irish banks is limited because of its membership with the European Union.

ISLE OF MAN

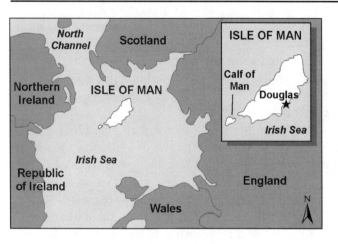

Overall rating: ★★★
Companies: ★★★
Trusts: ★★
Banking: ★★★★

Type of jurisdiction: No tax on foreign income.

Location: The Isle of Man is located in the Irish Sea between England, Scotland, and Ireland.

Population: Approximately 72,000.

Official language: English.

Currency: Pounds sterling, but U.S. dollars are prevalent in international business and investment.

Apart from a treaty with Britain, the Isle of Man is not party to any double-taxation treaties. The Isle of Man offshore financial services are attractive because of its —

- proximity to Europe,
- history of political and economic stability,
- well-developed telecommunications system and infra-structure,
- sophisticated company law, and
- lack of wealth, capital gains, and inheritance taxes.

Political and legal structure
The Lordship of Man was acquired in the 1760s by the British Crown, which ruled the Isle of Man until the islands separated from England in 1866. The governmental assembly is known as the Tynwald. It consists of an upper and lower house. The members of the houses are elected for five years and, with the British Crown, form the parliament of the Isle of Man. A chief minister is appointed by the governor on the nomination of the majority and holds office throughout the lifetime of each house.

The British government is responsible for overseas representation and defense, and an annual contribution is paid to that government for its services. Isle of Man law is based on English common law and much of the civil law legislation is modeled on the English Acts of Parliament.

Infrastructure and economy
Historically, Isle of Man's economy has been based on agriculture and tourism. Today, the economy is reliant on investment and its financial operations, which constitute more than 30% of the GDP. The Isle of Man has become a leader in the European tax haven industry.

The Isle of Man is served by a new airport and there are regular international flights. It has well-maintained roads.

Exchange control
There are no exchange controls in the Isle of Man.

Companies

Isle of Man companies are incorporated under the 1931 Companies Act. The act was originally based on the 1929 British Companies Act and has been amended significantly for offshore purposes. There are three types of companies available in the Isle of Man: private resident companies, nonresident companies, and exempt companies.

Private resident companies are used primarily by Isle of Man residents for carrying on business in the Isle of Man and are taxable. Nonresident companies are not taxable unless they operate in the Isle of Man or earn Isle of Man income other than bank interest. Exempt companies may be resident in the Isle of Man but are provided exemption from Isle of Man taxation upon payment of an exempt status fee and application to the government. An exempt company must have one resident director and a secretary, both of whom must be residents of the Isle of Man. It must also have a qualified accountant and lawyer.

An Isle of Man company may be incorporated under any name that is not considered undesirable by the registrar of companies, but words such as "Building Society," "Cooperative," "Chamber of Commerce," "Council Institute," "University," "Insurance," "Reinsurance," "Register," "Unit Trust," or "Investment Trust" are not permissible without the appropriate license. The Articles of Association govern the internal affairs of a company.

Trusts

Because of its association with the European Union, the Isle of Man is not a particularly strong jurisdiction in which to form trusts. Trusts (often referred to as Manx trusts) are governed by the trust laws of the Isle of Man. A Manx trust may be used to accumulate wealth for international clients and is not subject to taxation as long as the beneficiaries are not resident in the Isle of Man.

The discretionary trust is the most commonly used trust in the Isle of Man. Isle of Man trust deeds are not available for public inspection.

Banking

The Isle of Man has excellent banking facilities with clear policies. They include:

(a) Only quality institutions may establish themselves. Such institutions should usually already be supervised in another jurisdiction which may continue and coordinate with the Isle of Man supervision.

(b) Quarterly or half-yearly accounts are required as well as annual accounts.

(c) The minimum capitalization must meet Isle of Man requirements.

(d) Institutional ownership of license-holders is preferred.

(e) All beneficial ownership of over 5% in license-holders must be disclosed.

(f) At least two experienced people must be involved in the day-to-day administration of license-holders.

(g) There must be competent internal procedures.

(h) Accounts must be prepared by someone with appropriate indemnity insurance.

The Isle of Man distinguishes between domestic banking institutions and offshore managed banks.

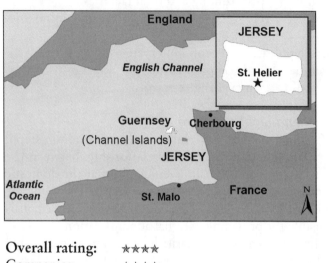

Overall rating: ★★★★
Companies: ★★★★
Trusts: ★★★
Banking: ★★★★

Type of jurisdiction: No tax on foreign income.

Location: Jersey is the largest of the Channel Islands, situated off the northwest coast of France near the Cherbourg Peninsula, in the Bay of St. Malo.

Population: Approximately 82,000.

Official language: English.

Currency: Pounds sterling, but U.S. dollars are prevalent in international business and investment.

Some of the reasons for the attractiveness of Jersey as a financial center are its —

- proximity to Europe,
- well-developed banking and legal facilities,
- excellent, reliable telecommunications and infrastructure,
- stable political and economic systems,
- well-developed company formation law, and
- lack of foreign exchange controls.

Political and legal structure

The Channel Islands have historically been administered by Britain. The constitutional relationship between the Channel Islands and Britain is unique in that the domestic government has the power to legislate on matters of domestic concern to the islands (including tax), while Britain is responsible for providing external administration.

At Jersey's request, the British government negotiated special arrangements with the European Union for Jersey under Article 227 of the Rome Treaty whereby Jersey is subject only to the customs union aspects of the Rome Treaty. Jersey is a common law jurisdiction.

Infrastructure and economy

International flights to and from Jersey are regular and reliable. Jersey has well-developed telecommunications networks and courier services. While the financial services sector provides Jersey's main source of income, the tourist industry continues to represent 45% of the island's GDP.

Exchange control

There is no exchange control in Jersey.

Companies

Only one type of company is available in Jersey, and it may be used for either private or public purposes. There are, however, two specific distinctions for tax purposes: income-tax status and exempt status. Income-tax status companies are not suitable for offshore purposes. Exempt status companies are exempt from Jersey income tax and pay only an annual exempt license fee. Both types of companies can be incorporated using any name that is not restricted by the Jersey authorities.

All Jersey companies must maintain a registered office in Jersey. There must be at least two directors who may be of any nationality, and a company secretary, who may be an individual or a corporation.

The share capital of a Jersey company must have a par value, but it may be of any amount and in any currency. Jersey law does not permit the use of bearer shares. The minimum number of shareholders is three, and they may be individuals or corporations of any nationality.

Trusts

Trusts have been constituted in large numbers in Jersey under general English common law principles. There is a significant amount of flexibility in the types of trusts that may exist in Jersey; the most common is the discretionary trust, which generally has powers of accumulation and advancement. Trusts may be either revocable or irrevocable. The Hague Convention was extended to Jersey in 1992 and affects offshore entities in Jersey

Banking

Jersey has poor bank secrecy laws but a strong and reputable banking industry. The banking act under the Depositors and Investors (Prevention of Fraud) Law contains many of the elements that are in the British Banking Act of 1987.

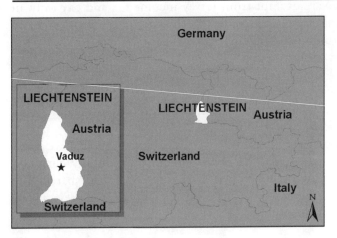

Overall rating: ★★★★
Companies: ★★★
Trusts: ★★
Banking: ★★★★

Type of jurisdiction: No tax; unique tax.

Location: Liechtenstein lies in the Upper Rhine, on the Austrian-Swiss border. Its capital is Vaduz.

Population: Approximately 30,000, most inhabitants living in Vaduz.

Official language: German. Alemannish, a dialect of German, is also spoken. English is also widely spoken.

Currency: Swiss francs, but U.S. dollars are prevalent in international business and investment.

Liechtenstein is considered one of the most sophisticated of all offshore centers. Its geographic location and excellent telecommunications are supported by highly efficient Liechtenstein banks and service industries. Liechtenstein's flexible company law provides for the formation of offshore holdings, domiciliary companies, foundations, and trusts.

Liechtenstein has opted not to become a member of the European Union.

Political and legal structure

Under the 1921 constitution, Liechtenstein has a hereditary prince and a democratically elected parliament. Liechtenstein has long enjoyed a stable political and economic climate and a strong currency. Liechtenstein banks, accountants, and lawyers enjoy a good reputation and a high degree of prestige worldwide. Liechtenstein operates on civil law principles.

Infrastructure and economy

Telecommunications are excellent in Liechtenstein and international courier services are well represented. Liechtenstein has no air services but can be reached by road or rail from Zurich in approximately two hours. Modern roads connect Vaduz with all nearby cities. The Rhine and Sarina Valleys are connected by a tunnel.

Liechtenstein's primary economy is the financial services sector.

Exchange control

No exchange controls apply to offshore entities operating out of Liechtenstein. However, under the currency treaty between Liechtenstein and Switzerland, any exchange controls introduced by Switzerland also apply to Liechtenstein.

Companies

The Liechtenstein Companies Act of 1926 governs offshore companies in Liechtenstein. There are two types of companies available. The first is the company limited by shares, or Aktiengesellschaft, which must submit annual audited accounts. It is subject to a 4% coupon tax on dividends and operates like a traditional IBC.

The second company formation is the establishment, or Anstalt, suitable only for one beneficial owner. Liechtenstein is also a suitable jurisdiction for the formation of foundations.

Trusts

Liechtenstein trust law is different from traditional trust law in that it does not prevent the accumulation of income nor does it have any rules against perpetuities. This allows for the creation of a trust with an unlimited duration. The trust deeds must specify whether or not commercial activities will be undertaken. This will determine whether auditors are required as are Liechtenstein companies.

Banking

The Banking Law of 1993 guarantees secrecy and applies not only to present and former bank staff but also to officials in the government. It can be overridden for the investigation of a crime. Liechtenstein has not joined the European Union in order to maintain its beneficial and confidential banking system.

LUXEMBOURG

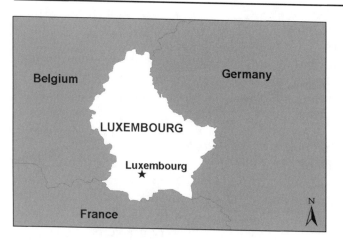

Overall rating: ★★★★
Companies: ★★★
Trusts: ★
Banking: ★★★★

Type of jurisdiction: Low tax.

Location: The Duchy of Luxembourg, a founding member of the European Union, is situated within the triangle where Belgium, Germany, and France meet. Its capital is Luxembourg City.

Population: Approximately 390,000.

Official language: German and French. English is also widely understood and spoken.

Currency: Luxembourg francs, but U.S. dollars are prevalent in international business and investment.

Luxembourg has become an important offshore financial center because of —

- the stability of its government,
- its well-educated, reliable work force,
- its central European geographic and time-zone location,
- its membership in the European Union, and
- the size and efficiency of its banking and professional sectors.

Political and legal structure

The Duchy of Luxembourg remained intact throughout the unification of the German states in the 19th century. Today Luxembourg is a constitutional duchy where the grand duke has similar powers to the queen of England. Democratic elections are held every five years.

Infrastructure and economy

Luxembourg's traditional economy was based on farming. Over the last 20 years, the banking and financial services sectors have grown substantially and are now the largest employer and the fastest-growing local industry. This evolution has established Luxembourg as an international financial center.

Luxembourg has the highest per capita GDP in Europe. Luxembourg City is the host of the European Court of Justice, the Secretariat of the European Parliament, the European Investment Bank, the European Court of Auditors, parts of the European Commission, and sections of North Atlantic Treaty Organization (NATO).

Luxembourg City's airport links Luxembourg with all major European capital cities. Luxembourg City is also linked by a well-developed network of highways and railways.

Exchange control
There are no exchange controls, although there is an obligation to disclose foreign currency transactions to the Luxembourg control authorities when Belgium is involved.

Companies
Three types of Luxembourg companies are generally used for offshore business:
(a) the 1929 traditional-style holding company
(b) the normal Luxembourg company with SOPARFI (normal taxable company with a restrictive holding company objective clause provision) provisions, sometimes known as the SOPARFI 990 holding
(c) the trading and commercial company

Both the 1929 traditional-style holding company and the normal Luxembourg company with SOPARFI provisions have become suitable for private investors and offshore business. Some of the particular attractions of these Luxembourg companies are listed below.

- Bearer or registered shares are allowed.
- Any currency can be used for minimum capital requirements.
- There is freedom from exchange control provisions.
- Access to the Luxembourg stock exchange is allowed for listing of the company's shares or bonds.
- Directors can be of any nationality.

The Luxembourg traditional-style holding company is most commonly used for —
- investments,
- management companies, and
- patents, trademark, and royalty reassignments.

In addition, a Luxembourg company with SOPARFI provisions can benefit from full double-tax treaty protection.

Trusts

There is no provision under Luxembourg law for trusts. However, it is possible to transfer assets to a bank that will administer them on your behalf according to a contract. Because of the lack of a trust law, the position of the settlor, trustee, and beneficiaries must be clearly set out in the contract.

Banking

Situated in the financial center of Europe, Luxembourg offers many advantages to international investors and offshore corporations. The country has a long history of political and economic stability, which has encouraged a solid banking sector, attracting the majority of the world's leading banking and financial institutions.

Luxembourg operates within a regulatory environment that protects the interests of the private sector and offers advantageous confidentiality laws for nonresidents which are strongly enforced, and which cover all financial institutions. Breaking banking secrecy is a criminal offense. For these reasons, Luxembourg has become an important center for international banking.

MADEIRA

Overall rating: ★★★
Companies: ★★★
Trusts: ★
Banking: ★★

Type of jurisdiction: No tax.

Location: Madeira comprises the islands of Madeira, Porto Santo, Deserta, and Selvagens. It is located in the Atlantic Ocean 600 miles (960 kilometers) southwest of Portugal.

Population: Approximately 275,000; of which about 100,000 live in the capital, Funchal.

Official language: Portuguese is the national language, but English is taught and therefore is widely used in commerce and international trade.

Currency: Portuguese escudos (PTE), which are held at PTE 160 = USD 1.

Madeira is a new and growing offshore jurisdiction. It is attractive for offshore financial services because of its:

- timely company availability,
- membership in the European Community,
- developed economic and professional infrastructure,
- reliable communications, and
- well-established banking system.

An extensive double-taxation treaty network makes Madeira an excellent location for the establishment of holding companies.

Political and legal structure

Madeira was colonized by the Portuguese in the 15th century. It achieved political independence in 1976 but still maintains a political unity with Portugal. The Madeiran Regional Parliament is an elected body that administers domestic interests such as the budget. Ultimate political power still resides with the central government in Lisbon, where Madeira has five elected representatives.

Infrastructure and economy

Funchal is Madeira's largest town and main port. The airport is one-and-a-half hours from Lisbon and three hours from most major European capital cities, many of which are served by direct flights.

Madeira also has a modern telecommunications system and a well-developed infrastructure.

Exchange control

All companies licensed to operate in the Free Trade Zone of Madeira benefit from complete freedom from exchange controls. The companies can operate using any currency, and they may freely transfer capital, profits, and funds.

Companies

There are two types of companies available: the private limited company and the Sociedad Anonima (SA) company. The SA company is the only company formation that can issue bearer shares; however, it is subject to certain controls, such as the auditing of financial accounts by a qualified auditor and the filing of audited accounts with the tax authorities and the public registry. The minimum number of shareholders is five, and the directors do not have to be Madeiran or Portuguese residents, but they may not be corporations. Companies require an annual limited review of the accounts that must be signed by the tax authorities.

The incorporation process for all companies is subject to name approval by the government. The object of the company must be specific and concise but may be altered. Companies must maintain a registered office in Madeira that also houses the statutory and accounting records together with supporting documents.

Trusts

Madeira is not a suitable jurisdiction for the formation of offshore trusts because of its civil law structure.

Banking

There is specific legislation covering bank secrecy in the Madeiran banking system, and there are both civil and criminal penalties for those convicted of breaches of confidentiality. Banking and financial services companies can operate as Portuguese companies in Madeira or as branches of foreign companies.

There are two types of offshore banking entities. They are subject to the same taxes as an onshore branch except that deposits from individuals who are nonresidents are not subject to the 20% withholding tax on the interest.

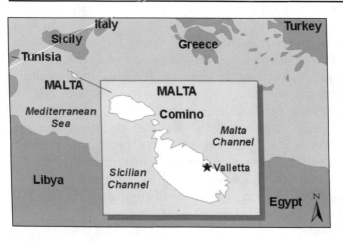

Overall rating: ★★★
Companies: ★★
Trusts: ★
Banking: ★★

Type of jurisdiction: Low tax.

Location: Malta is composed of three islands — Malta, Gozo, and Comino. The Maltese Islands are in the Mediterranean Sea, 62 miles (100 kilometers) south of Italy. The capital is Valletta.

Population: Approximately 380,000.

Official language: Maltese, although English is spoken by the majority of the population. Italian, French, and German are also used.

Currency: The Maltese lira, which is equivalent to approximately USD 2.40.

Malta became an independent country within the British Commonwealth in 1964. In 1987, Malta incorporated the European Convention on Human Rights and Fundamental Freedoms into its laws. This was the first legislation enacted in order to attract offshore business and has since been followed by significant changes of legislation governing various areas of financial services business.

Political and legal structure

Malta is a democratic republic with an elected parliament which consists of a president and a house of representatives. The house of representatives has a cabinet headed by a prime minister. Maltese law has its foundations in civil law, with some codes based on Napoleonic laws. Commercial and criminal law are largely modeled on British common law. The Malta Financial Services Centre promotes and regulates offshore business.

Infrastructure and economy

Malta has a very advanced telecommunications system. A new airport has been built to ensure comfort and efficiency for the increasing number of incoming and outgoing business professionals and tourists.

Tourism is a major part of the Maltese economy, and the country also maintains its traditional ship-building yards and ship-repairing docks.

Exchange control

Offshore companies are not subject to any foreign exchange control legislation.

Companies

Limited liability companies are set up under the Malta Financial Services Centre Act of 1988. Companies may be either public or private and must be formed by at least two entities. All Maltese companies are required to have a registered office in Malta. Any name is acceptable to the registrar but it must be approved and must end in "Limited." Offshore companies must be private Maltese companies with an object clause preventing them from conducting domestic Maltese business. They are, however, allowed to conduct business from Malta that does not concern Maltese domestic business. Offshore entities may not use Maltese currency.

An offshore company is required to have a nominee company as either the secretary or the company's sole director. A nominee company monitors the company's activities and holds pertinent information under a strict professional duty to maintain confidentiality.

Trusts

A valid Maltese trust is created by a written contract between the settlor and the trustee, which contains the name of the trust, its terms, and the names of the beneficiaries. The trust must be registered and the names mentioned in the contract cannot be altered without the consent of the court. When neither the settlor nor the beneficiaries are resident in Malta and the trust fund does not include Maltese immovable property, no taxes are payable on assets held by the trust.

Banking

Domestic banks are licensed under the Maltese Banking Act of 1994. Offshore banking is conducted from Malta in foreign currencies with nonresidents or with nonresident companies. Banks are subject to government supervision. Offshore banks must have a paid-up share capital of at least USD 1.5 million and must pay 5% income tax. Offshore banks are not taxed on dividends, transfer of profits abroad, or interest payments to nonresidents.

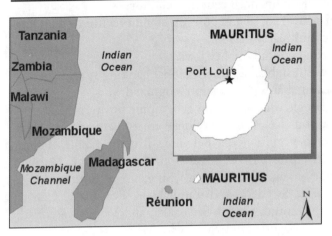

Overall rating: ✮✮✮
Companies: ✮✮
Trusts: ✮✮
Banking: ✮✮✮

Type of jurisdiction: No tax.

Location: Mauritius is an island of approximately 700 square miles (1,800 square kilometers) situated in the Indian Ocean, 500 miles (800 kilometers) east off the coast of Madagascar. The capital is Port Louis.

Population: Approximately 1.3 million.

Official language: English, although French and Creole are more commonly spoken.

Currency: Mauritian rupees (MUR), which are pegged to a variety of world currencies (presently MUR 18 = USD 1), but U.S. dollars are prevalent in international business and investment.

Mauritius has a number of features that make it an attractive offshore financial center, including —

- historical social and political stability within a democratic multiparty system,
- strong confidentiality laws,
- a well-established international banking system,
- bearer shares ownership recognized, and
- strategic time-zone and geographic position.

Mauritius has a well-developed treaty network. Favorable tax treaties exist with Belgium, Britain, China, France, Germany, India, Italy, Luxembourg, Madagascar, Malaysia, Namibia, Pakistan, Russia, Singapore, South Africa, Swaziland, Sweden, and Zimbabwe. Botswana, Canada, Kuwait, Lesotho, Oman, Sri Lanka, and Vietnam are in the process of negotiating treaties with Mauritius.

Political and legal structure

Mauritius was colonized by the Dutch in the 16th century. The Dutch left Mauritius in 1710 but left behind a developed sugar cane industry, which covered 90% of the land. The French subsequently occupied the island and named it Ile de France. In 1810, the island was captured by the British and the name Mauritius was reinstated. British rule lasted for 158 years, until 1968 when the Republic of Mauritius became an independent country and democracy within the British Commonwealth. Full executive power rests with the prime minister, who is head of the government. The president is the head of state, and the members of parliament are elected every five years.

Mauritius is a hybrid legal system based on British and French law. Company law is modeled on British corporate law.

Infrastructure and economy

Mauritius has a well-developed telecommunications infrastructure. Its strategic location facilitates communication with the Far East, Europe, and North America. International courier companies operate in Mauritius and provide prompt delivery services to most parts of the world. Airlines offer regular and direct flights between Europe and the Far East. Mauritius also has modern port facilities. The work force is well educated and has achieved a literacy rate of 90%.

Exchange control
Offshore entities are exempt from all exchange controls in Mauritius.

Companies
Mauritian offshore companies are governed by the Mauritian Companies Act of 1984, which is largely modeled on the British Companies Act of 1984. Mauritian offshore companies are required to be foreign owned and may not engage in domestic business or deal in the local currency. After an offshore company is incorporated, it may apply for its tax residence certificate so that it may be eligible to access the double-taxation treaties.

The name of the company may be anything as long as it is not already registered and does not include the words "State," "Government," "Authority," "Mauritius," "Municipal," "Cooperative," "Chamber of Commerce," or "Chartered." A profit-and-loss account and balance sheet must be filed annually with the government, and a registered office must be maintained in Mauritius with a minimum of two directors and a resident secretary. Offshore companies are also required to have a minimum of two shareholders unless all the issued shares are held by a holding company. Annual general meetings must be held every year.

Under the provisions of the Income Tax Act, Mauritian offshore companies are taxed at a fixed rate of 15%, while international companies are not taxed at all.

Trusts

Offshore trusts in Mauritius are governed by the Offshore Trusts Act of 1992. There is well-developed and flexible offshore trust legislation which ensures confidentiality and has been designed specifically to promote the establishment of asset protection trusts. Trusts are filed by notification of the government. The identity of the settlor and beneficiary are not required to be disclosed, but a local trustee must be appointed.

Banking

Mauritius has developed a solid banking and professional infrastructure. Provisions to allow offshore banking were introduced in 1988. Six major foreign banks have established branches in Mauritius and there are eight locally incorporated banks. Seven of the top ten global accounting firms are established in Mauritius and a small stock exchange exists. Mauritius is a member of the Offshore Group of Banking Supervisors.

Bank licenses are available in two types: domestic and offshore. Any type of banking institution may apply for either type of license. Banks must have a paid-up capital of at least MUR 25 million. In addition, a reserve equal to that amount must be maintained.

MONACO

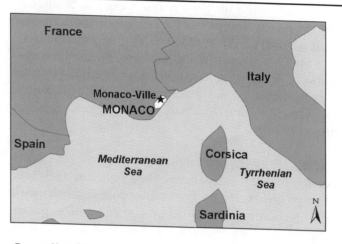

Overall rating: ★★★★
Companies: ★★★
Trusts: ★
Banking: ★★★

Type of jurisdiction: Unique tax.

Location: Monaco is situated on the French Mediterranean coast 12 miles (20 kilometers) west of Italy. Its capital is Monaco-Ville.

Population: Approximately 36,000.

Official language: French, although there is also a national Monegasque language. English and Italian are also frequently spoken.

Currency: French francs (FRF).

Monaco is an independent country, historically associated with France. It is well known for its well-developed, reliable banking and investment facilities and has been the offshore jurisdiction of choice for French and European businesses. Because of its association with France and the European Union, it is not typically used for company formation. As it operates under civil law, it is also not typically used for trust formation. Monaco's highly educated, professional citizens make doing business and investing from Monaco simple and cost-effective. Monaco has one of the highest standards of living in Europe.

Political and legal structure

Monaco has been an independent state since the 15th century. It does, however, have important economic links with France. The country is governed by a prince who appoints the ministers. The chief minister is appointed from a list of names compiled by the president of France, and legislation is made by an elected national council.

Infrastructure and economy

Monaco has a very well-developed infrastructure, and communication links are equivalent to France and on a par with major European cities. The economy is roughly divided between tourism (20%), banking and commerce (30%), general industry (10%), and services (40%).

Exchange control

Monaco is under the French exchange control for residents of Monaco and France. The government has recently attempted to make offshore transactions easier; thus, there is no exchange control on operations where funds are held outside Monaco or in a currency other than the French franc. It is anticipated that the removal of exchange control laws with the evolution of the European Community will boost Monaco's offshore sector.

Companies

Monaco's corporate law is modeled on that of France. Various types of companies are available, the most common being the Société Anonyme Monegasque (SAM). It can take several months to get permission to form such a company, and the name must not be the same as that of an existing company. Monaco law also requires the disclosure of the beneficial ownership of the company and that there be at least two shareholders. A qualified auditor must be appointed and at least two directors, one of whom must be a resident of Monaco. Once the company has been set up, it is possible to issue bearer shares. A company may not reduce its capital below FRF 500,000. General meetings must be held once a year and an office must be established in Monaco. It is possible for foreign companies to reside in Monaco.

Trusts

Trusts may not be formed in Monaco, but under the 1936 law, foreign trusts may be recognized. An existing trust may be transferred to Monaco provided that the same requirements that apply to the creation of a new trust are followed. Depending on the number of beneficiaries, tax may be applied to the trust. Trusts are also used by Monaco residents to avoid the Monegasque laws of succession.

Banking

All Monaco banks must first be established in France and banking is regulated by the Banque de France and the Comité des Etablissements de Credit. The principal attraction to establishing a bank in Monaco is that there is a relatively low rate of taxation.

A financial institution must appoint an auditor, and banks are required to have a minimum capital of FRF 15 million. Banks are subject to strong rules for the disposition of their assets and acceptable risks. For example, the total amount at risk must never exceed more than 20 times the bank's own funds. There must be sufficient liquid assets to meet all liabilities due within one month and the liquidity ratio must be reported quarterly.

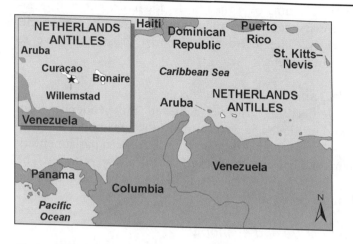

Overall rating: ★★★
Companies: ★★★
Trusts: ★
Banking: ★★

Type of jurisdiction: Low tax; unique tax.

Location: The Netherlands Antilles comprises two islands in the Caribbean off the north coast of Venezuela. The capital is Willemstad.

Population: Approximately 222,000.

Official language: Dutch, although English and Spanish are widely spoken.

Currency: Netherlands Antilles guilders (NAF), which have a constant value against the U.S. dollar so that NAF 1.79 = USD 1.00. U.S. dollars are prevalent in international business and investment.

The attractiveness of the Netherlands Antilles for offshore financial planning over the last decade has resulted in several countries reviewing their double-taxation agreements with them. The jurisdiction is now most attractive to European citizens.

Political and legal structure
The Netherlands Antilles achieved independence from Holland in 1954. The government functions under a democratic system which is derived from European parliamentary systems and has historically been politically very stable. The Netherlands Antilles enjoys a legal system based on the civil or Roman law system.

Infrastructure and economy
Curaçao is one of the most developed islands in the region, with a well-developed infrastructure. The main sources of income in the Netherlands Antilles are oil refinery, business in the free trade zone, the financial services industry, and tourism. The Netherlands Antilles enjoys associate status in the European Community.

Special tax provisions and tax treaties, particularly with the Netherlands, has attracted offshore entities to the islands. The offshore industry creates revenue for the Netherlands and generates considerable employment.

Exchange control
Exchange control is administered by the Central Bank of the Netherlands. An offshore company may obtain a license permitting freedom of currency transactions. To obtain this license the company must be owned by a nonresident using non–Netherlands Antilles currency and must not carry out domestic commercial activities.

Companies

The commercial code of the Netherlands Antilles regulates offshore company incorporation. Unlike most offshore jurisdictions, a declaration of no objection to the draft articles of incorporation must be obtained from the ministry of justice before incorporation. Once incorporated, an offshore company needs to obtain foreign exchange control exemption and a business license. The offshore company is prohibited from undertaking banking or insurance activities or investment business.

When entitled to offshore status, companies generally pay tax at 2.4% on profits of up to $60,000 and at 3% on profits above that amount.

Trusts

The Netherlands Antilles does not have attractive trust laws for offshore activities because of its civil law system.

Banking

The Netherlands Antilles are not an attractive jurisdiction for offshore banking activities because of the limited banking resources on the islands.

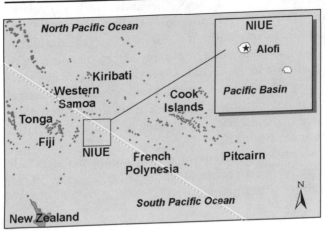

Overall rating: ★★
Companies: ★★★
Trusts: ★
Banking: ★★

Type of jurisdiction: No tax.

Location: Niue is known as the world's largest piece of coral. It is situated in the South Pacific between Samoa and the Cook Islands.

Population: Approximately 1,700, nine-tenths of which is of Polynesian descent. The other one-tenth of the population is of European or Tongan descent.

Official language: Polynesian, but the official commercial language is English.

Currency: New Zealand dollars (NZD). NZD 1.00 equals approximately USD 0.66. However, U.S. dollars are prevalent in international business and investment.

Niue is a relatively new and small offshore jurisdiction.

Political and legal structure
Niue is an independent territory associated with New Zealand. The Niue government is responsible for Niue's internal affairs while New Zealand is responsible for its external affairs. Niue is also a protectorate of Britain. The Niue assembly has 20 members, 14 of whom are elected by local constituencies and 6 by common roll. The head of government is the premier, who is elected by the assembly and who chooses the cabinet.

Infrastructure and economy
Most Niueans work on family farms and plantations. The economy of Niue is heavily dependent on aid from New Zealand. The agricultural sector consists mainly of gardening, although some cash crops are grown for export. Industry consists primarily of small factories to process passion fruit, lime oil, honey, and coconut cream. In recent years, a significant percentage of the population has emigrated to New Zealand.

Exchange control
No exchange controls exist in Niue.

Companies
The IBC is the only type of company available in Niue for international trade and investment. IBCs cannot trade within Niue or own property there. They cannot undertake banking, insurance, assurance, reinsurance, fund management, or asset management, and they cannot solicit the public for investment. An IBC has all the powers of a person.

A registered office must be maintained in Niue at the address of a licensed management company. Company names may not be registered if they are already in use or contain the words "Assurance," "Bank," "Building Society," "Chamber of Commerce," "Chartered," "Cooperative," "Imperial," "Insurance," "Municipal," "Royal," "Trust Company," or "Trustee Company." The words available for corporate endings are "Limited," "Corporation," "Incorporated," "Société Anonyme," "Sociedad Anonima," "Company," "Limitada," "Société par actions," and "Aktiengesellschaft." Niue IBC law denies the disclosure of beneficial ownership to authorities. Directors may be natural persons or corporations of any nationality and need not be residents of Niue. The minimum number of directors is one and the minimum number of shareholders is one. An IBC is exempted from local taxation.

Trusts
Nuie is not suitable for offshore trust structures.

Banking
Offshore banking business in Niue is licensed under the Offshore Banking Act and regulated by the Niue banking board. Offshore banking business is considered to be transactions carried on by persons and corporations not ordinarily resident or domiciled in Niue and not engaging in trade or business within Niue.

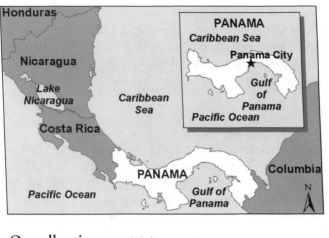

Overall rating: ★★★
Companies: ★★★
Trusts: ★★
Banking: ★★

Type of jurisdiction: No tax on foreign income.

Location: Panama is located between Costa Rica and Colombia. It forms the narrowest and lowest portion of the isthmus that links North and South America. The capital is Panama City.

Population: Approximately 2.4 million, half of which live in the major cities.

Official language: Spanish, but many people in Panama City and Colón speak English.

Currency: Balboa, which are on a par with U.S. dollars. U.S. dollars are prevalent in international business and investment.

Panama is an attractive offshore financial center because it offers —
- a simple and clear company formation process,
- nondisclosure of beneficial ownership assured in law,
- a moderately well-developed professional infrastructure,
- an established international banking system, and
- exemption from taxes on income earned outside Panama.

Political and legal structure
Panama was discovered in 1510, and Panama City was established in 1519. Originally a Spanish colony, in 1821 it became part of the Gran Colombia of Simon Bolivar. In 1903, Panama became an independent republic.

The executive branch of the government is composed of a president and two vice-presidents, all of whom are elected for a five-year term. The legal system is based on civil law.

Infrastructure and economy
Airlines operate through the international airport in Panama City. They provide service to all major cities in North, Central, and South America and Europe. Three ports in the country have facilities for shipping cargo and for accommodating regular ocean-going freighters and passenger ships. International telephone, telex, fax, and other telecommunications services are excellent. Courier services are available.

Exchange control
Offshore entities are exempted from exchange controls.

Companies
The most common corporate entity is the Sociedad Anonima, although other forms of legal entities can be formed (e.g., simple limited partnership, general partnerships, and stock-issuing limited partnerships). The corporation statute law

of 1927 is patterned on similar statutes taken from the United States. Since Panama is a civil law country, Panamanian corporations are principally regulated by the terms and conditions set out in the corporation's articles of incorporation.

A corporation's name must be approved and must not be the same as that of an existing Panamanian corporation. Words such as "Bank," "Trust," "Mutual Fund," "Insurance," and "Reinsurance" are not allowed unless licensed. There is no requirement to disclose the beneficial owners' names.

A Panamanian corporation must have a registered agent who is resident in Panama and who must be either a lawyer or a law firm. There must be at least three directors, one president, and a vice-president, along with a treasurer.

There is no minimum capital requirement, and the capital may be expressed in any currency. Shares may be issued with or without a par value. An annual registration tax is payable to the Panamanian government upon the anniversary of incorporation, and there are financial penalties for late payment.

Trusts

Panamanian trusts are set up under the Panamanian Law No. 1 of 1984. Under this law the trust —

- may have a maximum length of 80 years,
- must be created in writing,
- is deemed irrevocable unless declared to be revocable,
- must name the settlors, trustees, and beneficiaries,
- must describe the property subject to the trust,
- may not excuse the trustee from liability from gross negligence or willful misconduct,
- must be signed by an agent resident in Panama,
- need not be registered at the public registry unless the trust includes Panamanian property, and
- may provide for an alteration to the law.

Trustees and other administrative parties to the trust are subject to the supervision of the Panamanian Banking Commission. There is also an obligation of secrecy relating to the trusts or its transactions.

Banking

Although Panama has had limited legitimate banking facilities, recently the use of such banks has become more prominent. Banks in Panama are supervised by the Panamanian Banking Commission, and new banks are required to gain government approval and be licensed.

Panama has strict bank secrecy and has laws to prevent Panamanian banks from being used for money laundering. Although disclosure of beneficial ownership to senior bank officers is required, this information is protected by law. Criminal matters, of course, are exempt from the confidentiality laws.

ST. KITTS–NEVIS

Overall rating: ★★★
Companies: ★★★
Trusts: ★★★
Banking: ★★★

Type of jurisdiction: No tax.

Location: The islands of St. Kitts and Nevis are situated in the Caribbean.

Population: Approximately 12,000.

Official language: English.

Currency: Eastern Caribbean dollars (XCD), which are linked to U.S. dollars at the fixed rate of XCD 2.70 = USD 1.00, but U.S. dollars are prevalent in international business and investment.

There are a number of financial advantages to investing off-shore in Nevis —

- There is no taxation on a Nevis company's income, dividends, or distribution that is not earned in Nevis.
- Corporate financial returns are not required on an annual basis.
- Directors may be companies or individuals.
- Bearer share ownership is permitted.
- The company's principal office may be located anywhere in the world.
- Foreign companies may transfer domicile to Nevis or vice versa.

Political and legal structure

Nevis was a British colony until 1983. In 1983, it became independent and joined the Federation of St. Kitts–Nevis. Nevis is democratic and its government is based on the British parliamentary system with an elected local assembly. Its legal system operates on the common law system.

Nevis is exceptionally stable politically, and the government has instituted programs that have resulted in a low crime rate and full employment. The two political parties reflect this stability in that they are both centrist and do not have substantial philosophical differences.

Infrastructure and economy

Nevis has a state-of-the-art telecommunications network. The Nevis airport can accept only propeller aircraft, but there are indirect flights to the United States, Britain, and Canada. Tourism, sugar, and the offshore industry are the major sources of employment and income.

Exchange control

Offshore entities use currencies other than the Eastern Caribbean dollar and are exempt from exchange controls.

Companies

The Business Incorporation Act of 1984 governs the establishment of nonresident or offshore companies. The act is based on U.S. corporate laws.

A Nevis corporation can be incorporated with any name that is not already taken but may not include the words "Bank" or "Insurance." The name of the corporation must be suffixed with either "Corporation," "Incorporated," "Company," or "Limited."

The minimum number of directors allowed is three and they may be individuals or corporations of any nationality. There are no limits on the number of shareholders who may be individuals or corporations of any nationality. An annual general meeting is required to elect and appoint the directors.

All documents filed with the registrar of companies are available for public inspection; however, it is not necessary to file the names of the directors, officers, and shareholders.

Trusts

In 1994, Nevis adopted the Nevis International Trust Ordinance, a concise, clear, and flexible asset protection trust law designed to compete with that of the Cook Islands. The ordinance makes Nevis an attractive trust jurisdiction.

The aim of the Nevis trust laws are to allow foreign citizens to obtain protection against legal threats to their property and assets through asset protection trusts. Nevis courts will not recognize any foreign court orders regarding its domestic asset protection trusts, which forces foreign-judgment creditors to use local lawyers in Nevisian courts. This is often a costly and lengthy process. In addition, the Nevisian statute of limitations is limited to one year from the date of the trust creation.

Under Nevisian law, basic trust documents are not required to be filed with the Nevis government and trusts are not a matter of public record. The only public information needed to establish an asset protection trust is a standard form or letter naming the trustee, the date of trust creation, the date of the filing, and the name of the local trust company representing the trust.

Banking

Although Nevis has historically not been a strong banking jurisdiction, a number of the major banks are located there and the Offshore Banking Ordinance was created in 1996 to improve the country's attractiveness as an offshore banking jurisdiction. To qualify for an offshore banking license, a bank must be registered to do business in Nevis under the Banking Act. The bank must also be regulated by the Eastern Caribbean Central Bank or must be licensed in its jurisdiction of incorporation to accept deposits from members of the public.

SINGAPORE

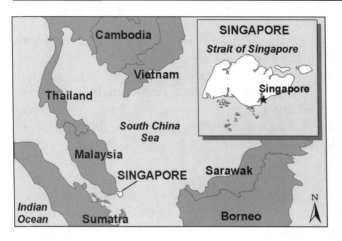

Overall rating: ★★★
Companies: ★★
Trusts: ★★
Banking: ★★★★

Type of jurisdiction: Unique tax.

Location: Singapore consists of an island and some 60 off-lying islands, which together total 240 square miles (615 square kilometers). It is located south of Malaysia and its capital is Singapore.

Population: Approximately 3 million.

Official language: Chinese, English, Malay, and Tamil. English is used primarily in commerce.

Currency: Singapore dollars, which float against a basket of currencies.

Singapore has not usually been considered a typical tax haven because it has relatively high tax rates. However, it does offer a number of advantages to offshore entities. The most important of these is its location in an area where, considering the uncertainties of the future of Hong Kong, international financial development is expanding. Singapore also has favorable tax laws for specific activities and beneficial rules for remitting income for Singapore-resident companies. Singapore also has a very favorable network of double-taxation treaties.

Political and legal structure

Singapore has been a British colony since 1867. In 1965, it became an independent republic within the British Commonwealth. A parliament is elected at least every five years. The parliament appoints the president, who then appoints the leader of the majority in parliament to be prime minister. The president also appoints the other ministers on the advice of the prime minister. The system of courts is based on English common law.

Infrastructure and economy

Singapore has a very well-developed telecommunications and transportation infrastructure with an international airport, developed roads, and one of the world's largest shipping ports.

The Singapore economy is heavily based on shipping and trade, as well as banking and financial services. Tourism, construction, technology, and manufacturing are also significant industries.

Exchange control

There are no exchange controls in Singapore.

Companies

Singapore company law comes from the Singapore Companies Act of 1967. The most common company type is one that is limited by shares, although it is also possible to have companies that are limited by guarantee or that are unlimited. Singapore companies may be either private or public. They are not typically formed for tax advantages.

Trusts

English common law influences the trust principles of Singapore law. The most significant differences from typical English common law are that there are no equivalents of the Perpetuities and Accumulation Act or of the Variation of Trust Act.

Banking

Most of the world's major banks are represented in Singapore, and banking is both reliable and efficient. Singapore is quickly gaining prominence as a major banking center in Southeast Asia, potentially replacing Hong Kong by the turn of the century.

Banks are licensed by the Monetary Authority of Singapore. They can be given either a full or restricted license. A restricted license may accept only certain types of deposits and offshore transactions. It is possible to have numbered accounts and thus retain banking confidentiality.

SWITZERLAND

Overall rating: ★★★★
Companies: ★★
Trusts: ★
Banking: ★★★

Type of jurisdiction: Low tax.

Location: Switzerland is in Europe, bordering Germany, Liechtenstein, Austria, Italy, and France. It covers approximately 15,625 square miles (40,000 square kilometers). Its capital is Berne.

Population: Approximately 7 million.

Official language: There are four national languages: German, French, Italian, and Romansch. Only the first three are official languages. English is widely spoken.

Currency: Swiss francs (CHF), which are divided into 100 cents each.

Switzerland is the most recognized and important offshore financial center in the world and has been the banking and offshore jurisdiction of choice for major corporations and wealthy individuals during the 20th century. However, in recent years it has become much less attractive as an offshore jurisdiction.

Switzerland is a mature offshore center; its banking system has become cumbersome and complex. Its treaties have made it less advantageous than some other jurisdictions, and it has a large number of double-taxation agreements. Switzerland does not have the bold guarantees of total confidentiality that are found in some of the newer offshore centers. Despite this, Switzerland continues to provide a high level of confidentiality, although it will divulge information in cases involving criminal activity.

Political and legal structure

The Swiss constitution dates from 1848. Switzerland is governed at three levels: the federal level is responsible for defense, foreign affairs, currency, postal services, telecommunications, and criminal law; cantons are responsible for education and policing and appoint their own magistrates; local matters are dealt with at a communal level.

Switzerland has a civil law system that is based on a number of traditions including the French and the Austrian civil codes.

Infrastructure and economy

Switzerland has an exceptionally well-developed telecommunications and transport infrastructure. It is easily accessible from around the world. Its economy is based primarily on financial and banking services.

Exchange control

Offshore entities are not subject to exchange controls in Switzerland.

Companies

While there are no simple corporate structures (such as tax-free IBCs) available in Switzerland, the Swiss company law is based on the Federal Code of Obligations, 1936. Indeed, since the formal introduction of anti-treaty shopping laws and other provisions starting in 1962, the environment for the use of such offshore companies has altered. Some offshore corporate possibilities, however, are still available, such as —

- private limited company by shares (Aktiengesellschaft),
- public limited company (Aktiengesellschaft), and
- private limited company — without shares (Gesellschaft mit beschrankter Haftung).

Trusts

Because Switzerland's legal system is based on civil law, it does not have a trust law, although there have been cases where the Swiss courts have considered and recognized trusts. Since 1984, Switzerland has been a party to the Hague Convention on the law applicable to trusts.

Banking

The Swiss banking system has been one of the preeminent banking systems in Europe, and it has been the backbone of Switzerland's position in the offshore world. Switzerland has a central bank, but banks are overseen by the Federal Banking Commission.

Many foreign banks have branches in Switzerland. This is because —

- the country is stable,
- it has good bank secrecy,
- it is one of the world's largest banking centers,
- many international clients requiring banking facilities and portfolio management view Switzerland as geographically and politically convenient, and
- it is possible to raise loan money relatively inexpensively.

TURKS AND CAICOS ISLANDS

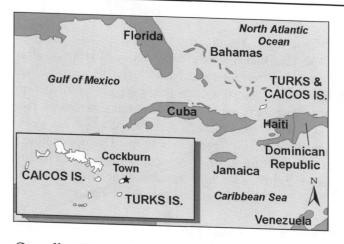

Overall rating: ★★★
Companies: ★★★
Trusts: ★★★
Banking: ★★

Type of jurisdiction: No tax.

Location: The Turks and Caicos Islands are located near the Bahamas and consist of six inhabited islands totaling 166 square miles (425 square kilometers). The capital is Cockburn Town.

Population: Approximately 20,000.

Official language: English.

Currency: U.S. dollars.

Turks and Caicos has in recent years become a more widely used offshore jurisdiction, mainly for Canadians. However, it has had some government scandals that have tarnished its image.

Political and legal structure

Until 1962, the islands were a dependency of Jamaica, after which time they were associated with the Bahamas. Since 1973, they have formed a completely separate jurisdiction under the British crown. The government consists of two houses. The lower house has 20 seats, 13 of which are elected by universal suffrage every five years. The upper house consists of a chief minister, four members appointed by the governor, and three ex-officio members, including the governor. Turks and Caicos has a common law system.

Infrastructure and economy

Turks and Caicos has relatively modern telecommunications systems. The airport offers international flights on a regular basis, and there is a developed domestic infrastructure.

The economy is primarily based on fishing and farming activities which support the local population, with most products being imported. Tourism is the largest industry. In 1984, Turks and Caicos introduced the Companies Ordinance, which was amended in 1989 to provide the exempt company.

Exchange control

Offshore entities are not subject to exchange controls in Turks and Caicos.

Companies

Turks and Caicos companies are formed under the Companies Ordinance of 1981-1994. The concepts are based on British corporate law, although the ordinance contains a wide array of features designed for offshore purposes. Usually, companies that are formed for the purpose of doing business in Turks and Caicos are known as ordinary companies, while those that are formed for the purpose of offshore activities (i.e., whose main business will be outside Turks and Caicos) are known as IBCs.

In 1993, the option of limited life companies also became available. This allows IBCs to become limited life companies and to be treated as such under U.S. tax law. Therefore, shareholders may be taxed as partners, while the company itself is not subject to any tax. Three other corporate vehicles are available in Turks and Caicos, but they are uncommon —

- the exempted limited life company,
- the guarantee company, and
- the hybrid company.

Trusts

Because of its British heritage, the trust law of Turks and Caicos is well recognized. The principal law is the Trusts Ordinance of 1990, which has been modeled on Jersey trust law. The ordinance is not an exhaustive edit of the British law and the British principles continue to apply only as long as there are no overriding statutory provisions. The Hague Convention on trust law was extended to apply to Turks and Caicos in 1993.

Banking

While Turks and Caicos has a strong environment for the creation of banks, it has a very poor banking system and there are only two banks in the jurisdiction. Banks are regulated under the Banking Ordinance of 1979.

GLOSSARY

Accumulation

Accumulation is the process of letting income earned build up indefinitely in the trust.

Asset protection

Asset protection involves restructuring the ownership and control of assets so as to protect them from business, corporate, and personal risks.

Asset protection trust

An asset protection trust is a trust structure specifically designed to protect your assets from lawsuits and creditors and to shelter the assets from any type of attack. If properly structured and used with an IBC, asset protection trusts can also provide other advantages such as tax reduction and third-party legal ownership.

Bearer shares

Bearer shares are a means of ownership common to many IBCs. Bearer shares differ from regular shares in that they are not registered in a person's name and the holder of the bearer shares owns the IBC. If the bearer shares are placed in trust, then the trust owns the IBC. Bearer shares provide a simple way of transferring ownership and a high level of anonymity.

Beneficiary

A beneficiary is the individual or corporation that will ultimately receive the trust assets or profit, as the trust document specifies.

Capital gains tax

Capital gains tax is a government tax on profit earned from the sale or disposition of a capital asset (e.g., land or shares).

Capitalization

Capitalization refers to the value or market worth in money of the initial assets or money placed in a corporate or trust structure.

Captive insurance

Captive insurance insures certain risks for a limited number of clients and is provided by a private insurance company. Captive insurance companies reduce insurance expenditure or can provide coverage where coverage may not otherwise be available.

Civil law

Civil law is a legal system derived from an early Roman concept, based on the code of law. Some offshore jurisdictions use this legal system.

Common law

Common law is a legal system derived from an early English concept, based on precedents determined by the courts. Many offshore jurisdictions use this legal system, and it is also the model of law in Canada and the United States.

Corporate bank account

A corporate bank account is an account in a company's name that is owned and controlled by that company. Any number of individuals may have signing authority to execute transactions on the account.

Corporation

A corporation is a legal entity structured according to the laws of the jurisdiction in which it is incorporated.

It is a distinct legal entity from the individual or corporations that incorporate it.

Director

Most corporations have directors who are responsible for management decisions of the corporation's activities and who act pursuant to corporate resolutions adopted by the directors or the shareholders who authorize business activities undertaken by the corporation. Offshore corporations may or may not have directors that take on such roles.

Double-taxation treaty

An agreement between two or more countries that outlines how taxes must be allocated and remitted to the government of each when business is done in both countries or when a nonresident or resident earns personal income in those countries.

Estate planning

Estate planning is the process of organizing assets so that you can pass them on to your successors in a desired way and often in a tax-advantageous manner.

Estate taxes

Estate taxes are levied on inherited assets or assets which are passed on after the original owner dies.

Exchange control

An exchange control is a currency control preventing or limiting the fluctuation of a particular country's currency against another currency (usually the U.S. dollar). An exchange control can also restrict currency conversion.

Exempt company

An exempt company, like an IBC, is not subject to tax in the jurisdiction in which it is incorporated. Exempt companies exist in jurisdictions that do not have IBCs. Specific forms of exempt companies may exist to offer specific advantages (such as access to tax treaties) in jurisdictions that do not have IBCs.

Family limited partnership

A family limited partnership is a form of partnership available in the United States which, if properly structured, offers tax advantages and limited liability.

Foundation

A foundation is a permanent organization funded to provide financing for specific purposes or beneficiaries.

GDP

Gross domestic product: the total value of all the goods and services produced in a country by both nationals and non-nationals during a specified period (e.g., a year).

Hague Convention

The Hague Convention is an agreement adopted through the Hague Conference of Private International Law to unify the rules of private international law. This is primarily done through multilateral treaties and conventions in fields of international law such as: recognition of companies; solving conflicts between jurisdictions; recognition and enforcement of foreign judgments, wills, estates, or trusts; and international judicial and administrative cooperation. Eighteen sessions of the Hague Conference have taken place since 1893. The last one was in October 1996 and regular plenary sessions have been scheduled every four years.

With minor exceptions, none of the jurisdictions known as offshore are signatories to the Hague Convention, which can subsequently exercise very little influence over these jurisdictions. Check with an international-law lawyer for more details.

International business company (IBC)

An international business company, or IBC, is a type of offshore corporation structured in jurisdictions that have advantageous corporate laws for asset protection, estate planning, and tax planning. Different jurisdictions use different forms of IBCs.

Jurisdiction

A jurisdiction is a country or recognized political subdivision of a country that has jurisdictional authority and the power to administer law, such as specific international business law, tax law, asset protection law, estate planning law, corporate law, and/or trust law. These laws may be beneficial for international and offshore purposes.

Limited liability company

A limited liability company's incorporating documents (and the governing laws of the jurisdiction under which it is formed) limit the liability of that company to its assets or specific assets associated with the company. The personal assets of shareholders, directors, or employees of the company are not exposed to creditors of or lawsuits against the company.

Limited life companies

A limited life company is a company whose incorporating documents have a specified life span.

Nominee director

The nominee director is a person who fills the role of director required by a country's incorporation laws. Sometimes a corporation takes on this role.

Offshore

Offshore refers to foreign financial centers in any country. However, offshore is most commonly used to describe tax havens or low-tax countries. It can also refer to the practice where some or all of an investor's financial activities are in a jurisdiction other than where the investor lives.

Offshore structure

An offshore structure is one or more legal entities established to hold direct ownership and/or control of property, cash, or other assets.

Par Value

Par value is the value of an investment security printed on its face. For example, a share may have a par value of $1 but may trade at any amount.

Partnership

A partnership is the relationship which exists between persons carrying on business in common with a view to profit. It is not a legal entity separate from its individual partners and as such, the liability in a partnership is not limited to the assets of the partnership but may include the personal assets of the partners.

Personal bank account

A personal bank account is an account in an individual's name, owned and controlled by that individual.

Power of attorney

Power of attorney is a written document in which one party empowers another to represent him or her or to act in his or her place for certain purposes. For example, it can give an individual or corporation the right to access another person's or entity's assets, and/or to transact business in relation to those assets.

Principal

A principal is the owner of a legal entity. The principal is usually a person, but can sometimes be a corporation.

Probate

Probate is the legal process used to validate a will and charge fees based on the value of the estate.

Protector

A protector is an individual or corporation specified in a trust document that is given certain powers and duties, usually to approve or veto the decisions of a trustee. A protector provides some assurance that the trustee will act in conjunction with the settlor's or beneficiary's wishes. The particular powers can be amended and edited in the trust document.

Reporting laws

Reporting laws are laws that specify when individuals and corporations must report worldwide assets, investments, profits, or transactions.

Separate legal entity

An individual or corporation that owns an asset and is legally definable as distinct from any other entity. The definition and determination of control and ownership is very important in tax planning, asset protection, and estate planning.

Settlor

A settlor is the individual or corporation that originally creates and transfers the initial assets, investments, or property into a trust.

Shareholder

A shareholder is an individual or corporation that holds ownership in a company through shares.

Statute of limitations

The statute of limitations specifies the time limit during which a legal action can be taken. Beyond the statute of limitations, legal actions cannot be raised.

Structuring offshore

Structuring offshore is a process of setting up legal entities that can conduct business or hold ownership and/or control of property, cash, or other assets offshore or internationally.

Tax evasion

Tax evasion is an illegal use of methods and/or mechanisms to avoid payment of taxes and/or the failure to pay such taxes.

Tax haven

Tax haven is another term for offshore center. It is a foreign financial center or jurisdiction that has advantageous tax laws.

Treaty

A treaty is an agreement between two (or more) countries outlining the terms of mutual assistance, mutual benefit, or disclosure for a specific purpose (e.g., avoidance of double taxation on the same income).

Trust

A trust is an equitable or fiduciary obligation binding one person, the trustee, to deal with the subject matter of the trust (any form of property), under his or her control and legal ownership for the benefit of one or more others, the beneficiaries.

It is a means of separating legal ownership from beneficial ownership, or ownership from enjoyment. The trust is a legal concept recognized almost without exception in common law countries, including countries that have been subject to British influence in the past.

Trustee

A trustee is an individual or corporation that oversees the trust and ensures the trust is administered as per the trust document. This is usually a licensed trust company or entity that meets the requirements of the specific jurisdiction's trust laws.

Withholding tax

Withholding tax is a tax held back at the source from payments or income, and is used to satisfy government requirements (e.g., advance payment on income tax). It is frequently used when foreign individuals or corporations are involved in a transaction.

To receive a free catalogue, please write to the nearest address listed below:

IN THE U.S.A.
Self-Counsel Press Inc.
1704 N. State Street
Bellingham, WA 98225

IN CANADA
Self-Counsel Press
1481 Charlotte Road
North Vancouver, BC V7J 1H1

or

Self-Counsel Press
4 Bram Court
Brampton, ON L6W 3R6

Visit our Web site at www.self-counsel.com